Super Cute

25 Amigurumi Animals

Super Cute

25 Amigurumi Animals

Annie Obaachan

BARRON'S

A QUANTUM BOOK

First edition for the United States, its territories and possessions, Canada, and the Philippines published in 2009 by Barron's Educational Series, Inc.

All inquiries should be addressed to:
Barron's Educational Series, Inc.
250 Wireless Boulevard
Hauppauge, New York 11788
www.barronseduc.com

ISBN-10: 0-7641-4297-6
ISBN-13: 978-0-7641-4297-0

Library of Congress Control Number: 2009925846

This book is published and produced by
Quantum Books
6 Blundell Street
London N7 9BH

QUMCUTE

Printed and bound in China

9 8 7 6 5 4 3 2 1

Design: Paula Keogh
Photographer: John Gaffen
Editor: Sarah Stubbs
Publisher: Anastasia Cavouras

Contents

Cute, Cute, Cute: Welcome to the Wonderful World of Amigurumi   6

Tools and Materials   8

Techniques   10
     Reading Patterns   11
     Crochet Techniques   12
     Fastening Off   18
     Designing Your Own Animals   20

Chapter 1: World of Pets   22

Chapter 2: Into the Wild   82

Chapter 3: In the Ocean   102

Chapter 4: Flippers and Wings   112

Chapter 5: In the Garden   122

Resources   140

Index   142

Cute, Cute, Cute

Welcome to the Wonderful World of **Amigurumi**

What Is Amigurumi?

The word *amigurumi* is a combination of the words *ami* and *nuigurumi*. *Ami* means "knit/crochet" in Japanese and *nuigurumi* means "stuffed toy." Put them together, and you have a crocheted stuffed toy.

No one really knows where amigurumi came from. There have always been handmade toys in Japan. Japan also has a rich history in textiles, as we can see in weaving for kimonos, the Japanese traditional costume. But there is no such history of knitting or crochet. The Japanese simply took these Western crafts, and instead of using them for purely functional items like socks and scarves, started to create little animals. Nowadays there are hundreds of amigurumi exhibitions and clubs, not only in Japan but all over the world.

The birth of amigurumi may have been greatly influenced by Japanese traditional doll culture, which has a long history. Hina Matsuri, a doll festival in honor of Girls' Day is celebrated on the third March, every year, just in time for the peach blossoms. The Odairi-sama/Ohina-sama dolls, representing the Emperor and the Empress, are displayed for this festival by each family with a daughter to ensure her future happiness. This set of dolls tends to be handed down from generation to generation with love, respect, and a sense of history. Boys also have a special doll festival in May.

The dolls stay with Japanese children all their lives, lifting their spirits in times of stress and trouble. Amigurumi animals are an extension of this doll culture, brightening up cloudy days and providing comfort at the toughest of times.

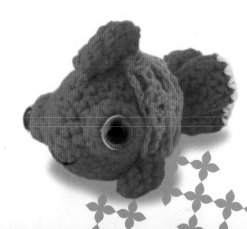

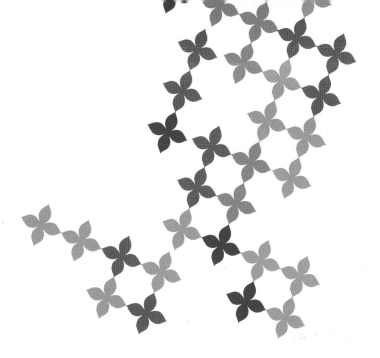

The last few years have witnessed a flowering of Japanese subcultures worldwide. A particularly popular feature of this phenomenon is the Japanese "kawaii"culture. The closest translation of *kawaii* in English is "cute." From Hello Kitty to Pokémon, anime to manga, cute Japanese characters have swarmed across the world and conquered our hearts. Amigurumi creations also swam with this kawaii-tide. Small, cute, and easy to make, how could they fail to captivate us?

In Japan, people like to keep these animals with them throughout the day. You will see them hanging off bags next to lucky charms, or sitting atop computers and piles of work in the office. Amigurumi characters can comfort and reassure us in this hectic world, secretly saying, "Why don't you take a little break and relax?"

Anyone can master amigurumi, and there are no limits to what you can create. Grab some yarn and crochet hooks, get comfortable by the fire, and start making your own little world.

Tools and Materials

Basic Crochet Kit

Crochet hooks come in a great variety of materials — from wooden and plastic to steel, and even ivory — and in different shapes and sizes. Always double-check that you are using the correct size hook as indicated in the pattern.

Knitter's pins with large heads (useful for pinning shapes).

Blunt-ended needle for sewing up.

Split stitch markers for marking the beginnings of rounds.

Tape measure

Sharp scissors

Tweezers to help with stuffing.

Embroidery needle for embroidering faces and details.

Embroidery thread

Craft wire or pipe cleaners for parts that need more shaping.

Well-spun yarns are the best to achieve neat, tidy work.

Fine crochet cotton (lace) thread has a firm texture that is good for beaks. Its thickness is given in numbers, i.e., 5, 10, and so on. The higher the number, the finer the thread.

Fingering yarn is good to have, especially for making smaller animals.

Worsted/Sportweight yarn is good for making large animals, but make sure the crochet is as tight as possible, so the stuffing can't be seen. You can achieve different results in amigurumi depending on the size or type of yarn you use, even when you are working on the same pattern. The thicker the yarn, the bigger your amigurumi will be!

Glass eyes and noses for facial adornments.

Batting for stuffing your animals.

Felt

Scraps of yarn to use as scarves or patches to dress up the amigurumi.

Techniques

Reading Patterns

If this is the first time that you have used crochet patterns, you might feel like you are learning a new language. However, you will soon begin to recognize the abbreviations used in crochet. The abbreviations make patterns shorter and easier to follow.

Let's learn the new crochet language.

Crochet Abbreviations

alt	alternate
approx	approximately
beg	begin/beginning
bet	between
ch	chain stitch
cm	centimeter(s)
col	color
cont	continue
dc	double crochet
dc2tog	double crochet 2 stitches together
dtr	double treble crochet
dec	decrease/decreasing/decreases
foll	follow/follows/following
hdc	half double crochet
inc	increase/increases/increasing
mm	millimeter
rep	repeat(s)
sc	single crochet
sk	skip/miss
sl st	slip stitch
st(s)	stitch(es)
tog	together
tr	treble
yo	yarn over hook
*	repeat the step

Hook Sizes

Now, it's time to step into the hook-sizing world.

Both letters and numbers appear on the packaging of most hooks. The metric sizing is the actual measurement of the hook. The letter is the U.S.

sizing range. Lettering may vary, so always rely on the metric sizings.

How to read a Japanese crochet chart

METRIC	USA
2.5 mm	B
3 mm	C
3.25 mm	D
3.5 mm	E
4 mm	F
4.25 mm	G
5 mm	H
5.5 mm	I
6 mm	J
7 mm	K
8 mm	L
9 mm	M
10 mm	N
15 mm	P
16 mm	Q
19 mm	S

On the Japanese chart, each stitch is shown as follows:

Magic ring: tiny circle in the middle of circular chart
Single crochet: cross
Chain stitch: tiny oval
Triangle: increasing
Triangle: decreasing
Slip stitch: black oval

Follow the chart from the center to the outside, then move to the non-circular part of the chart, if there is one shown above the circular one. Always follow the chart counter-clockwise.

Crochet Techniques

Crochet is all about mixing really simple techniques with more elaborate flourishes. Once you get the hang of making chains, you are ready to progress to a variety of fancy stitches.

Holding the hook and yarn

Learning how to hold the hook and yarn correctly is the first step to crochet. Most people hold the hook and yarn as they would a pencil or a knife, but you should experiment to find the most comfortable way for you.

Mastering the slipknot

Making a slipknot is the first step in any project. Master the slipknot technique, and you are on your way to super crochet!

Make a loop in the yarn. With your hook, catch the ball end of the yarn and draw it through the loop. Pull firmly on the yarn and hook to tighten the knot and create your first loop.

Making a chain

1. Before making a chain, you need to place the slipknot on a hook. To make a chain, hold the tail end of the yarn with the left hand and bring the yarn over the hook by passing the hook in front of the yarn, under, and around it.

2. Keeping the yarn taut, draw the hook and yarn through the loop.

3. Pull the yarn, hook it through the hole, and begin again, ensuring that the stitches are fairly loose. Repeat to make the number of chains required. As the chain lengthens, keep hold of the bottom edge to maintain tension.

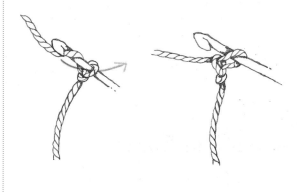

How to count a chain

To count the stitches, use the right side of the chain, or the side that has more visible and less twisted "V" shapes, as shown. Do not count the original slip stitch (sl st), but count each "V" as one chain.

Making a slip stitch (sl st)

A slip stitch (sl st) is used to join one stitch to another or a stitch to another point, as in joining a circle, and is usually made by picking up two strands of a stitch. However, when it is worked into the starting chain, only pick up the back loop.

1. Insert the hook into the back loop of the next stitch and pass yarn over hook (yo), as in the chain (ch) stitch.

2. Draw yarn through both loops on stitch and repeat.

The magic ring: working in the round

There are two ways to start circular crochet. One is with a chain and another is with a loop. The loop, or magic ring, is the more common way to make amigurumi. This way of working in the round ensures that there is no hole in the middle of the work, as there is with a chain ring, because the central hole is adjustable and can be pulled tightly closed.

Let's make a magic ring

This will be the first round of your amigurumi, so you need to master it!

1. Make a loop by wrapping the yarn twice onto your forefinger, with the tail end of the yarn on the right, the ball end on the left.

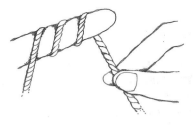

2. Pull the ball end through the loop (steady your work with your hand).

3. Make one chain (ch) through the loop on the hook you have drawn through to steady the round.

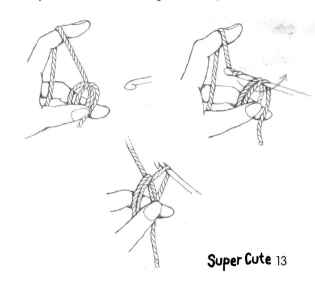

4. Work as many single crochets (sc), or whatever stitch you are using, into the loop as is required by the pattern.

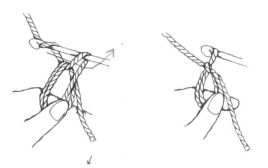

5. Pull the last stitch out long enough so that it won't come undone. Find out which loop will be tightened first by pulling one of the loops.

6. Pull this loop as tight as you can.

7. Pull the tail end of the yarn to tighten up the whole loop. Now you have no hole in the middle of the first round.

Completing the magic ring: first round

Insert the hook into the first stitch of a magic ring and pull the yarn through all the way.

This is called "slip stitch" (sl st).

Starting the second round

To crochet a flat circle, you need to keep working in the round with increasing stitches.

1. Make one chain (ch). Insert the hook into the first stitch of a circle, put the yarn over the hook (yo), and then draw the yarn through loop. This is called single crochet (sc). In amigurumi, this is the technique you will use the most.

2. Add one more sc into the same stitch. This is called increasing (inc).

Repeat 1 and 2 into every stitch and you will finish the second round with twice the number of stitches.

On the second round, increase in alternate stitches.

Third round: 1sc into each of the next 2 stitches, 2sc into the next one. Repeat.

Fourth round: 1sc into each of the next 3 stitches, 2sc into the next one. Repeat.

The more rounds you go, the more stitches you need to make between increases.

Making a chain ring

1. Work a chain as long as required by the pattern.

2. Join the last chain (ch) to the first with a slip stitch (sl st). Begin the first round by working into each chain stitch.

Variety of stitches

Single crochet (sc): This will be the main stitch used for amigurumi.

1. Insert the hook, front to back, into the next stitch. Yo.

2. Draw through one loop to front; there should be two loops on the hook. Yo.

3. Draw through both loops to complete single crochet.

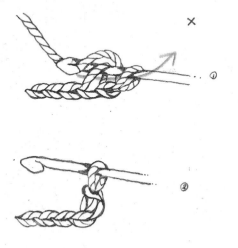

Double crochet (dc)

This makes a more open fabric as the stitches are taller.

1. Yo from back to front. Insert the hook into the next stitch, from front to back. Yo again and draw through the stitch.

2. There should be three loops on the hook. Yo and pull through two loops. Yo and draw through first two.

3. There should be two loops on the hook. Yo. Pull through the remaining two loops to complete. Yo and draw through last two to complete double crochet.

Half-double (hdc)

The half-double is simply that: half of a double crochet. Therefore, the stitch is slightly shorter than double crochet. In step 2 of double crochet, pull through all the remaining loops in one movement.

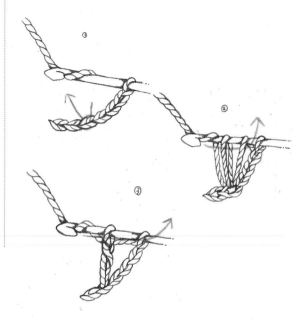

Fastening Off

If you want your little animal to be perfect, fastening off is the most important step — and also the most nerve-wracking. The key to success in every amigurumi project is perfect assembly.

Here are some useful things to remember:

When you fasten off the ends of the arms and legs, leave a long tail for sewing the pieces together. Do not weave this end in.

Connect two pieces by taking stitches alternately from each piece and fastening them securely to each other.

Fastening off

1. After fastening off the last stitch, snip off the yarn from the ball, leaving a couple of inches to weave in.

2. Draw through the last loop, pulling tightly to fasten.

Weaving in ends

1. Use the hook to draw the yarn through at least five stitches, weaving the yarn over and under as you go to secure the yarn and ensure it does not work free.

2. Snip off the excess yarn.

Designing Your Own Animals

This book contains 25 step-by-step projects, but once you have mastered these patterns and had some practice, you may wish to start designing your own little creatures. There are no rules for designing amigurumi. You just need a little time, patience, and lots of enthusiasm. The main ingredient is your imagination.

Sketching

Use the world around you for inspiration.

Start by sketching whatever you see. Inspiration is everywhere: your dog waiting for his meal and looking up at you with big round eyes, your cat chasing a ball endlessly, or a hippo constantly yawning in the zoo. Sketch anything you find interesting. Don't worry about your drawings being too neat — these are just your design ideas and can be as messy as you want.

Developing your design

Once you've finished a few sketches, it's time to develop the design! The first thing to decide is what the basic features of your animal are going to be — for example, its posture, colors, texture, character, and size. Amigurumi animals can be as realistic or as stylized as you like.

Deciding on the shape of your animal is like playing with blocks! Almost all amigurumi amimals are made of combinations of certain shapes. These include ball shapes, egg shapes, sausage shapes, half spheres, almond shapes, tubes, and many more. Experiment and play with the shapes until you find the right combination. Keeping a set of various types of crocheted shapes just for this purpose is helpful.

Making shapes with circular crochet

Flat disc

To create a flat circle, either in spirals or by joining, work two stitches into each stitch in the first round, then into every other stitch in the following round, every third stitch in the third round, and so on till you reach the diameter you require. You can work either in spiral or by joining the first st and the last st with sl st at each round.

Sphere

To make a 3-D round shape, you need to increase the diameter. Work a few rounds even before decreasing. Work two stitches into each stitch in the first round, then every other stitch in the following round, and every third stitch in the third round. Keep straight for 2 to 4 rounds before decreasing stitches. Work two stitches together with every third stitch in this round, and then two stitches together with every alternate stitch in the next round, and so on.

Egg shape

To make the fat end of the egg, increase in every stitch in the first round, every alternate stitch in the second round, every third stitch in the third round, and every fourth stitch in the fourth round. Keep straight for one or two rounds, then decrease gradually as before, but with a straight round between each decreasing round.

Sausage

This is similar to making a sphere. After the initial increasing round, keep straight for the length required, then decrease the round as before.

Half sphere

Make this just like the sphere but fasten off at the halfway stage.

Working in the round means no turning, so it's easy to lose which round you're on. Consider stitch markers as little helpers. They will remind you where you started. There are two ways of working in the round. You can either work in spirals, or join the last stitch of each round by a slip stitch to the first stitch.

Choosing yarn

Experimenting with different types of yarn and fibers will help you create an exciting range of textures. It is a good idea to tape samples of yarn next to your sketches. One of the joys of the process is finding new materials to use.

Facial expression

You can use your creatures' facial expressions to convey a variety of moods and personalities. You can make them look jolly, grumpy, or sleepy. Don't worry about creating realistic features; in amigurumi, the more exaggerated the better.

Drawing a few lines across your face sketches is a good way to find the expression you would like to use. Divide a face into 4 sections and experiment with different positions for the eyes, nose, and mouth. Moving the position of these features slightly will make a surprising difference.

Changing the ratio of head size to body size can also result in dramatic changes to the look of your creatures.

Chapter 1
World of Pets

Puppies! Floppy Ears

With his super-floppy ears, this guy is so cute! You can make his ears as big and as floppy as you want.

Materials

Hook size: 3mm

Eyes: 8mm

Plastic nose

Brown yarn

Red yarn for accessories

Batting

Head

Use brown yarn.

Make a loop with the tail end of the yarn on the right, keeping the ball end on the left.

Pull the ball end through the loop. Make one ch through the loop on the hook you have drawn through to steady the circle. 6sc into the circle and complete with sl st into the first sc.

1st round: 2sc into each of 6sc. (12st)

2nd round: *1sc. 2sc into next sc. *6 times (18st)

3rd round: *1sc into each of next 2sc, 2sc into next sc. *6 times (24st)

4th–7th round: 1sc into every sc.

8th round: *1sc into each of next 2sc, skip 1, 1sc. *6 times (18st)

9th round: *1sc, skip 1, 1sc. *6 times (12st)

Insert batting.

10th round: *1sc, skip 1, *6 times (6st)

Fasten off.

Tail

Start the same way as you did for the head, but with 3sc into the circle.

1st round: 2sc into each of 3sc. (6 st)

2nd–10th round: 1sc into every sc.

Fasten off.

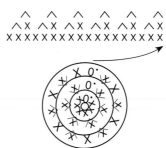

Body

Start the same way as you did for the head.

1st round: 2sc into each of 6sc. (12st)

2nd round: *1sc. 2sc into next sc. *6 times (18st)

3rd round: *1sc into each of next 2sc, 2sc into next sc. *6 times (24st)

4th–8th round: 1sc into every sc.

9th round: *1sc into each of next 2sc, skip 1, 1sc. *6 times (18st)

10th round: *1sc, skip 1, 1sc. *6 times. (12st)

Insert batting.

11th round: *1sc, skip 1. *6 times (6st)

Fasten off.

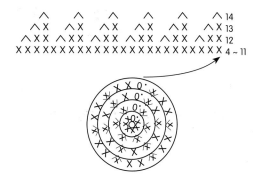

Floppy ears x2

Start the same way as you did for the head.

1st round: 2sc into each of 6sc. (12st)

2nd–4th round: 1sc into every sc. (12st)

5th round: *1sc. 2sc into next sc. *6 times (18st)

6th–7th round: 1sc into every sc. (18 st)

8th round: *1sc into each of next 2sc, 2sc into next sc. *6 times (24st)

9th–12th round: 1sc into every sc.

13th round: *1sc into each of next 2sc, skip 1, 1sc. *6 times (18st)

14th–17th round: 1sc into every sc. (18st)

18th round: *1sc, skip 1, 1sc. *6 times (12st)

19th–20th round: 1sc into every sc.

21st round: *1sc, skip 1. *6 times (6st)

Fasten off.

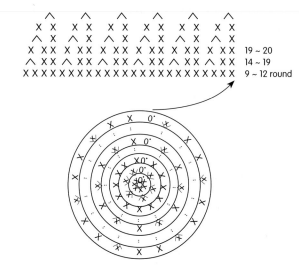

Nose

Start the same way as you did for the head, but with 3sc into the circle.

1st round: 2sc into each of 3sc. (6st)

2nd round: *1sc, 2sc into the next sc. *3 times (9st)

3rd round: *1sc into next 2sc, 2sc into the next sc. *3 times (12st)

4th–5th round: 1sc into every sc. (12st)

Fasten off.

Legs (Back) x2

Start the same way as you did for the head.

1st round: 2sc into each of 6sc. (10st)

2nd round: *1sc. 2sc into next sc. *6 times (15st)

3rd round: 1sc into every sc. (15st)

4th round: *1sc into next 3sc, skip 1, 1sc. *3 times (12st)

5th–7th round: 1sc into every sc. (12st)

8th round: *1sc into next 3sc. 2sc into the next sc. *3 times (15st)

9th round: *1sc into next 2sc. 2sc into the next sc. *5 times (20st)

10th–12th round: 1sc into every sc. (20st)

13th round: *1sc into the next 2sc, skip 1, 1sc. *5 times (15st)

14th round: *1sc, skip 1, 1sc. *5 times (10st)

Insert batting.

15th round: *1sc, skip 1. *5 times (5st)

Fasten off.

Legs (Front) x2

Start the same way as you did for the head, but with 5sc into the circle.

1st round: 2sc into each of 5sc. (10st)

2nd round: *1sc. 2sc into the next sc. *5 times (15st)

3rd–5th round: *1sc into every sc. (15st)

6th round: *1sc into next 3sc, skip 1, 1sc. *3 times (12st)

7th–12th round: 1sc into every sc. (12st)

Insert batting.

13th round: *1sc, skip 1. *6 times (6st)

Fasten off.

Hat

Use red yarn.

Start with making 6sc into the ring, joining the first sc and the last one with sl st.

1st round: 2sc into each of 6sc. (12st)

2nd round: 1sc into each stitch.

3rd round: 1sc into every other stitch. (6st)

Fasten Off.

Scarf

Use red yarn.

Make ch to the length of scarf your floppy ears would like to wear.

Hdc to the end.

Fasten off.

Making Up

Sew all parts together as shown in the photograph.

Attach the eyes and nose.

Sew on the hat and the scarf.

Puppies! Fluffy Fur

With his fluffy fur, this puppy is perfect for cuddling. Use fine mohair when you make him for extra, extra softness.

Materials

Hook size: 3mm

Eyes: 8mm

White mohair yarn

Brown mohair yarn for patches

Plastic nose

Ribbon

Batting

Head

Use white yarn.

Make a loop with the tail end of the yarn on the right, keeping ball end on the left.

Pull the ball end through the loop. Make one ch through the loop on the hook you have drawn through to steady the circle. 6sc into the circle and complete with sl st into the first sc.

1st round: 2sc into each of 6sc. (12st) with white.

2nd round: *1sc, 2sc into next sc. *6 times (18st), twice with white yarn, once with brown, once more with white, once more with brown, and finish with white for last stitch.

3rd round: *1sc into each of the next 2sc, 2sc into the next sc. *6 times (24st). Keep changing the col when you come to the position where you changed the col in the previous round.

4th–7th round: 1sc into every sc.

8th round: *1sc into each of next 3sc, 2sc into next sc. *6 times (30st)

9th round: *1sc into each of next 4sc, 2sc into next sc.* 6 times (36st). Break off brown, then continue in white.

10th–11th round: 1sc into every sc.

12th round: *1sc into each of next 4sc, skip 1, 1sc. *6 times (30st)

13th round: *1sc into each of next 3sc, skip 1, 1sc. *6 times (24st)

14th round: *1sc into each of next 2sc, skip 1, 1sc. *6 times (18st)

15th round: *1sc, skip 1, 1sc. *6 times (12st)

Insert batting.

```
 ^     ^     ^      ^      ^        ^       16
 ^x    ^x    ^x     ^x      ^x       ^x      15
^xx   ^xx   ^xx    ^xx     ^xx      ^xx     13
^xxx  ^xxx  ^xxx   ^xxx    ^xxx     ^xxx    12
xxxxxxxxxxxxxxxxxxxxxxxxxxxxxxxxxxxxxxxx    10 ~ 11
```

16th round: *1sc, skip 1. *6 times (6st)

Fasten off.

Body

Start the same way as you did for the head.

1st round: 2sc into each of 6sc. (12st)

2nd round: *1sc. 2sc into next sc. *6 times (18st)

3rd round: *1sc into each of next 2sc, 2sc into next sc. *6 times (24st)

4th round: * 1sc into each of next 3sc, 2sc into next sc. *6 times (30st)

5th–8th round: 1sc into every sc.

9th round: *1sc into each of next 3sc, skip 1, 1sc. *6 times (24st)

10th round: *1sc into each of next 2sc, skip 1, 1sc. *6 times (18st)

11th round: *1sc, skip 1, 1sc. *6 times (12st)

Insert batting.

12th round: *1sc, skip 1. *6 times (6st)

Fasten off.

Legs x4

Start the same way as you did for the head.

1st round: 2sc into each of 6sc. (12st)

2nd round: *1sc. 2sc into next sc. *6 times (18st)

3rd–10th round: 1sc into every sc.

11th round: *1sc, skip 1, 1sc. *6 times (12st)

Insert batting.

12th round: *1sc, skip 1. *6 times (6st)

Fasten off.

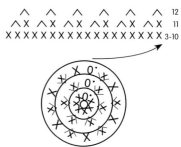

Ears x2

Start the same way you did for the head, but with 4sc into the circle.

1st round: 2sc into each of 4sc. (8st)

2nd–10th round: 1sc into every sc.

Fasten off.

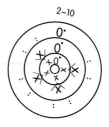

Nose

Start the same way as you did for the head.

1st round: 2sc into each of 6sc. (12st)

2nd round: *1sc. 2sc into next sc. *6 times (18st)

3rd–5th round: 1sc into each sc.

Fasten off.

Tail

Start the same way as you did for the head, but with 3sc into the circle.

1st round: 2sc into each of 3sc. (6st)

2nd–10th round: 1sc into every sc.

Fasten off.

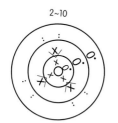

Making Up

Sew all parts together as shown in the photograph.

Attach the eyes and nose.

Tie on the ribbon in a color of your choice.

Puppies! Wagging Tail

This puppy with his wagging tail is always pleased to see you. Dress him in a different color neckerchief every day for some variety.

Materials

Hook size: 3mm

Eyes: 8mm

Cream or beige yarn

White yarn

Fabric

Black embroidery thread

Batting

Head

Use cream yarn.

Make a loop with the tail end of the yarn on the right, keeping the ball end on the left.

Pull the ball end through the loop. Make one ch through the loop on the hook you have drawn through to steady the circle. 6sc into the circle and complete with sl st into the first sc.

1st round: 2sc into each of 6sc. (12st)

2nd round: *1sc. 2sc into next sc. *6 times (18st)

3rd round: *1sc into each of next 2sc, 2sc into next sc. *6 times (24st)

4th round: *1sc into each of next 3sc, 2sc into next sc. *6 times (30st)

5th round: *1sc into each of next 4sc, 2sc into next sc. *6 times (36st)

6th–10th round: 1sc into every sc.

11th round: *1sc into each of next 4sc, skip 1, 1sc. *6 times (30st)

12th round: *1sc into each of next 3sc, skip 1, 1sc. *6 times (24st)

13th round: *1sc into each of next 2sc, skip 1, 1sc. *6 times (18st)

14th round: *1sc, skip 1, 1sc. *6 times (12st)

Insert batting.

15th round: *1sc, skip 1. *6 times (6st)

Fasten off.

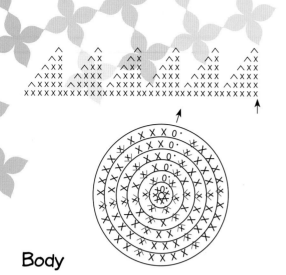

Body

Start the same way as you did for the head.

1st round: 2sc into each of 6sc. (12st)

2nd round: *1sc, 2sc into next sc. *6 times (18st)

3rd round: *1sc into each of next 2sc, 2sc into next sc. *6 times (24st)

4th–9th round: 1sc into every sc.

10th round: *1sc into each of next 2sc, skip 1, 1sc. *6 times (18st)

11th round: *1sc, skip 1, 1sc. *6 times (12st)

Insert batting.

12th round: *1sc, skip 1. *6 times (6st)

Fasten off.

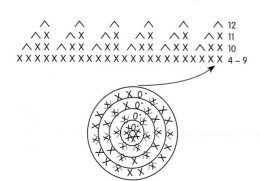

Ears x2

Start the same way as you did for the head, but with 4sc into the circle.

1st round: 2sc into each of 4sc. (8st)

2nd round: *1sc, 2sc into next sc. *4 times (12st)

3rd–4th round: 1sc into every sc.

Fasten off.

Legs x4

Start the same way as you did for the head, but with 5sc into the circle.

1st round: 2sc into each of 5sc. (10st)

2nd–7th round: 1sc into every sc.

Insert batting.

8th round: *1sc, skip 1. *5 times (5st)

Fasten off.

Tail

Start the same way as you did for the head, but with 3sc into the circle.

1st round: 2sc into each of 3sc. (6st)

2nd–10th round: 1sc into every sc.

Fasten off.

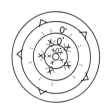

Nose

Use white yarn.

Start the same way you did for the head.

1st round: 2sc into each of 6sc. (12st)

2nd–3rd round: 1sc into every sc.

Insert batting.

Fasten off.

Making Up

Sew all parts together as shown in the photograph.

Embroider the mouth and nose with black embroidery thread.

Attach the eyes.

Sew on the neckerchief.

Cute Kitten

This kitten is so tiny she can fit inside a teacup! Could she be any cuter? Pick nice, soft cream-colored wool to make her.

Materials

Hook size: 3mm

Eyes: 8mm

Cream yarn

Pink round button

Pink embroidery thread

Batting

Head

Make a loop with the tail end of the yarn on the right, keeping the ball end on the left.

Pull the ball end through the loop. Make one ch through the loop on the hook you have drawn through to steady the circle. 6sc into the circle and complete with sl st into the first sc.

1st round: 2sc into each of 6sc. (12st)

2nd round: *1sc, 2sc into next sc. *6 times (18st)

3rd round: *1sc into each of next 2sc, 2sc into next sc. *6 times (24st)

4th round: *1sc into each of next 3sc, 2sc into next sc. *6 times (30st)

5th–9th round: 1sc into every sc.

10th round: *1sc into each of next 3sc, skip 1, 1sc. *6 times (24st)

11th round: *1sc into each of next 2sc, skip 1, 1sc. *6 times (18st)

12th round: *1sc, skip 1, 1sc. *6 times (12st)

Insert batting.

13th round: *1sc, skip 1. *6 times (6st)

Fasten off.

Body

Start the same way as you did for the head.

1st round: 2sc into each of 6sc. (12st)

2nd round: *1sc, 2sc into next sc. *6 times (18st)

3rd round: *1sc into each of next 2sc, 2sc into next sc. *6 times (24st)

4th–8th round: 1sc into every sc.

9th round: *1sc into each of next 2sc, skip 1, 1sc. *6 times (18st)

10th–11th round: 1sc into every sc.

Insert batting.

12th round: *1sc, skip 1, 1sc. *6 times (12st)

Fasten off.

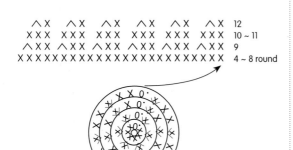

Ears x2

Start the same way as you did for the head, but with 3sc into the circle.

1st round: 2sc into each of 3sc. (6st)

2nd round: *1sc, 2sc into next sc. *3 times (9st)

3rd round: *1sc into each of next 2sc, 2sc into next sc. *3 times (12st)

Fasten off.

Tail

Start the same way as you did for the head, but with 5sc into the circle.

1sc into each of 5sc to 5cm.

Fasten off.

Making Up

Sew all parts together as shown in the photograph.

Attach the eyes and nose.

Embroider the mouth with pink embroidery thread.

Crazy Kitten

When she sees a ball of wool, this kitty can't help herself, she goes crazy! Sometimes she gets so excited she gets all tangled up in the wool. If you don't like red, you can use blue, yellow, green, or purple for her ball of wool.

Materials

Hook size: 3mm

Eyes: 8mm

Light gray yarn

Yellow and black embroidery thread

Batting

Head

Make a loop with the tail end of the yarn on the right, keeping the ball end on the left.

Pull the ball end through the loop. Make one ch through the loop on the hook you have drawn through to steady the circle. 6sc into the circle and complete with sl st into the first sc.

1st round: 2sc into each of 6sc. (12st)

2nd round: *1sc, 2sc into next sc. *6 times (18st)

3rd round: *1sc into each of next 2sc, 2sc into next sc. *6 times (24st)

4th round: *1sc into each of next 3sc, 2sc into next sc. *6 times (30st)

5th round: *1sc into each of next 4sc, 2sc into next sc.* 6 times (36st)

6th–9th round: 1sc into every sc.

10th round: *1sc into each of next 4sc, skip 1, 1sc. *6 times (30st)

11th round: *1sc into each of next 3sc, skip 1, 1sc. *6 times (24st)

12th round: *1sc into each of next 2sc, skip 1, 1sc. *6 times (18st)

13th round: *1sc, skip 1, 1sc. *6 times (12st)

Insert batting.

14th round: *1sc, skip 1. *6 times (6st)

Fasten off.

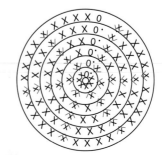

Body

Start the same way as you did for the head.

1st round: 2sc into each of 6sc. (12st)

2nd round: *1sc, 2sc into next sc. *6 times (18st)

3rd round: *1sc into each of next 2sc, 2sc into next sc. *6 times (24st)

4th–7th round: 1sc into every sc.

8th round: *1sc into each of next 4sc, skip 1, 1sc. *4 times (20st)

9th–16th round: 1sc into every sc.

17th round: *1sc into each of next 2sc, skip 1, 1sc. *5 times (15st)

18th–19th round: 1sc into every sc.

20th round: *1sc, skip 1, 1sc. *5 times (10st)

Insert batting.

21st round: *1sc, skip 1. *5 times (5st)

Fasten off.

Legs and Arms x4

Start the same way as you did for the head, but with 5sc around the circle.

1st round: 2sc into every sc. (10st)

2nd–15th round: 1sc into every sc.

16th round: *skip 1, 1sc. *5 times (5st)

Insert batting.

Fasten off.

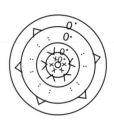

Tail

Start the same way as you did for the head, but with 4sc around the loop to start.

1st round: 2sc into every sc. (8st)

2nd round: 1sc into every sc until it is long enough for a tail.

3rd round: *skip 1, 1sc. *4 times

Fasten off.

Ears x2

Start as you did for the head, but with 3sc into the circle.

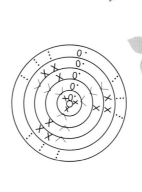

1st round: 2sc into each of 3sc. (6st)

2nd round: *1sc, 2sc into next sc. *3 times (9st)

3rd round: *1sc into each of next 2sc, 2sc into next sc. *3 times (12st)

4th–5th round: 1sc into every sc.

Fasten off.

Making Up

Sew all parts together as shown in the photograph.

Attach the eyes.

Embroider the nose and mouth with yellow embroidery thread, and the toes with black embroidery thread.

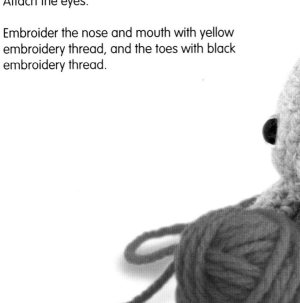

Bad Budgies

This budgie has been very bad. He's been flying around the house causing all sorts of trouble, but now he's sitting on his perch pretending to be good as gold. Have fun making lots of bad budgies in a rainbow of colors.

Materials

Hook size: 3mm

Eyes: 6mm

Yellow (or light blue) yarn

Light green (or purple) yarn

Yellow cotton fine crochet thread

Black/pink/blue embroidery thread

Batting

Body colors in parentheses ( ) are for alternative colorway

Use yellow (light blue) yarn.

Make a loop with the tail end of the yarn on the right, keeping the ball end on the left.

Pull the ball end through the loop. Make one ch through the loop on the hook you have drawn through to steady the circle. 6sc into the circle and complete with sl st into the first sc.

1st round: 2sc into each of 6sc. (12st)

2nd round: *1sc, 2sc into next sc. *6 times (18st)

3rd round: *1sc into each of next 2sc, 2sc into next sc. *6 times (24st)

4th–8th round: 1sc into every sc.

9th round: Change to light green (purple) yarn. 1sc into every sc.

10th round: *1sc into each of next 3sc, 2sc into next sc. *6 times (30st)

11th–19th round: 1sc into every sc.

Back tail section

20th row: 1sc into next 12sc.

21st row: 1ch, 2sc tog, 1sc into every sc except last 2sc, 2sc tog. (10st)

22nd row: 1ch to start, 1sc to end.

23rd row: 1ch, 2sc tog, 1sc into every sc except last 2sc, 2sc tog. (8st)

24th row: 1ch to start, 1sc to end.

25th row: 1ch, 2sc tog, 1sc into every sc except last 2sc, 2sc tog. (6st)

26th row: 1ch to start, 1sc to end.

27th row: 1ch, 2sc tog, 1sc into every sc except last 2sc, 2sc tog. (4st)

28th–31st row: 1ch to start, 1sc to end.

32nd row: 1ch, 2sc tog, 1sc into every sc except last 2sc, 2sc tog. (2st)

Insert batting.

33rd–36th row: 1ch to start, 1sc to end.

Fasten off.

Go back to working in the round for the rest of the body.

Attach the yarn to 1st st on the back tail and work 1sc into each st to the end. Cont in the round.

20th round: 1sc into every sc.

21st round: *1sc into each of next 3sc, skip 1, 1sc. *6 times (24st)

22nd round: *1sc into each of next 2sc, skip 1, 1sc. *6 times (18st)

23th round: *1sc, skip 1, 1sc. *6 times (12st)

Insert batting.

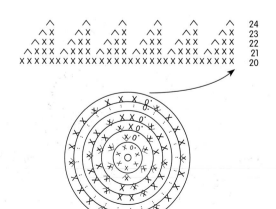

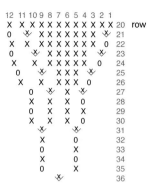

24th round: *1sc, skip 1. *6 times (6st)

Fasten off.

Wings

Section A x2

Use yellow yarn (light blue).

Start the same way as you did for the body.

1st round: 2sc into each of 6sc. (12st)

2nd round: Make 1ch to start. 1sc into the first sc. 2sc into each of next 4sc, 1sc into next sc, join to the first sc with sl st.

3rd round: Make 1ch, 1sc into each of next 2sc, 2sc into each of next 6sc, 1sc into next 2sc, join to the first sc with sl st.

4th–5th round: 1sc into every sc.

Fasten off.

Section A

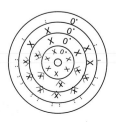

Section B x4

Use light green yarn (purple).

Start the same way as you did for the body.

1st round: 2sc into each of 6sc. (12st)

2nd round: Make 1ch to start. 1sc into the first sc. 2sc into each of next 4sc, 1sc into next sc, join to the first sc with sl st.

3rd round: Make 1ch, 1sc into each of next 2sc, 2sc into each of next 6sc, 1sc into next 2sc, join to the first sc with sl st.

4th round: 1ch, 1sc into each of next 4sc, 2sc into each of next 8sc, 1sc into each of next 4sc, join to the first sc with sl st.

5th round: Make 1ch, 1sc into each of next 6sc, 2sc into next sc, 1sc into each of next 4sc, 2sc into next 2sc, 1sc into each of next 4sc, 2sc into next sc, 1sc into each of next 6sc, join to the first sc with sl st.

Fasten off.

Sew this pointy circle shape in half.

Section B

Beak

Hook size: 2mm

Use yellow fine crochet thread.

Start the same way as you did for the body, but with 3sc into the circle.

1st round: 2sc into every sc. (6st)

2nd round: *1sc, 2sc into next sc. *3 times (9st)

3rd–5th round: 1sc into every sc.

Fasten off.

Making Up

Sew the wings onto the body.

Attach the eyes.

Embroider the feet with yellow embroidery thread; the black dots on the face with black embroidery thread; and the nose bridge with blue (pink) embroidery thread to make your budgies look super cute!

Bouncing Bunnies

These super-sweet bunnies like to give out chocolate eggs at Easter, but even more than that, they love eating them! Have fun creating their floppy ears and their little round tummies.

Materials

Hook size: 3mm

Eyes: 8mm

Cream yarn

Gray yarn

White mohair

Black embroidery thread

Batting

Head

Use cream yarn.

Make a loop with the tail end of the yarn on the right, keeping the ball end on the left.

Pull the ball end through the loop. Make one ch through the loop on the hook you have drawn through to steady the circle. 6sc into the circle and complete with sl st into the first sc.

1st round: 2sc into each of 6sc. (12st)

2nd round: * 1sc, 2sc into next sc. *6 times (18st). Start inserting gray yarn for patches (as for puppy on p. 28).

3rd round: *1sc into each of next 2sc, 2sc into next sc. *6 times (24st)

4th round: *1sc into each of next 3sc, 2sc into next sc. *6 times (30st)

5th–7th round: 1sc into every sc.

8th round: *1sc into each of next 3sc, skip 1, 1sc. *6 times (24st)

9th round: *1sc into each of next 2sc, skip 1, 1sc. *6 times (18st)

10th round: * 1sc, skip 1, 1sc. *6 times (12st)

Insert batting.

11th round: *1sc, skip 1. *6 times (6st)

Fasten off.

Body

Use cream yarn.

Start the same way as you did for the head.

1st round: 2sc into each of 6sc. (12st)

2nd round: *1sc, 2sc into next sc. *6 times (18st). Start inserting gray yarn for patches.

3rd round: *1sc into each of next 2sc, 2sc into next sc. *6 times (24st)

4th round: *1sc into each of next 3sc, 2sc into next sc. *6 times (30st)

5th–10th round: 1sc into every sc.

11th round: *1sc into each of next 3sc, skip 1, 1sc. *6 times (24st)

12th round: *1sc into each of next 6sc, skip 1, 1sc. *3 times (21st)

13th–15th round: 1sc into every sc.

16th round: *1sc into each of next 5sc, skip 1, 1sc. *3 times (18st)

Insert batting.

17th–19th round: 1sc into every sc.

Fasten off.

Tummy

Use white mohair.

Start the same way as you did for the head.

1st round: 2sc into each of 6sc. (12st)

2nd round: *1sc, 2sc into next sc. *6 times (18st)

3rd round: *1sc into each of next 2sc, 2sc into next sc. *6 times (24st)

4th round: *1sc into each of next 3sc, 2sc into next sc. *6 times (30st)

5th round: *1sc into each of next 4sc, 2sc into next sc. *6 times (36st)

Fasten off.

Nose

Use cream yarn.

Start the same way as you did for the head.

1st round: 2sc into each of 6sc. (12st)

2nd–3rd round: 1sc into every sc.

Fasten off.

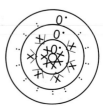

Cheeks x2

Use white mohair for fluffy texture.

Start the same way as you did for the head, but with 5sc into the circle.

1st round: 2sc into each of 5sc. (10st)

2nd–3rd round: 1sc into every sc.

Fasten off.

Legs x2

Use cream yarn.

Start the same way as you did for the head.

1st round: 2sc into each of 6sc. (12st)

2nd round: *1sc, 2sc into next sc. *6 times (18st)

3rd–5th round: 1sc into every sc.

Insert batting.

Fasten off.

Arms x2

Use cream yarn.

Start the same way as you did for the head, but with 5sc into the circle.

1st round: 2sc into each of 5sc. (10st)

2nd–4th round: 1sc into every sc.

5th round: *1sc into each of next 3sc, skip 1, 1sc. *Twice. (8st)

6th–9th round: 1sc into every sc.

Insert batting.

Fasten off.

Feet x2

Use cream yarn.

Start the same way as you did for the head.

1st round: 2sc into each of 6sc. (12st)

2nd–6th round: 1sc into every sc.

7th round: *1sc into each of next 2sc, skip 1, 1sc. *3 times (9st)

8th–10th round: 1sc into every sc.

Fasten off.

Ears x2

Use gray yarn.

Start the same way as you did for the head, but with 4sc into the circle.

1st round: 2sc into each of 4sc. (8st)

Work 1sc into every sc in round until you get 4.5cm.

Fasten off.

Making Up

Sew all parts together as shown in the photograph.

Attach the eyes.

Embroider claws and nose with black embroidery thread.

Rat Attack

When this little rat doesn't get enough attention, he gets, well, ratty! But with his dainty pink paws and cute snout, he usually gets what he wants. Use very fine pink thread for his ears, hands, and feet.

Materials

Hook sizes: 2mm and 3mm

Eyes: 6mm

Gray yarn

Pink fine crochet thread

Fine wire for tail

Batting

Head

Make a loop with the tail end of the yarn on the right, keeping the ball end on the left.

Pull the ball end through the loop. Make one ch through the loop on the hook you have drawn through to steady the circle. 6sc into the circle and complete with sl st into the first sc.

1st round: 2sc into each of 6sc. (12st)

2nd round: *1sc, 2sc into next sc. *6 times (18st)

3rd round: *1sc into each of next 2sc, 2sc into next sc. *6 times (24st)

4th–7th round: 1sc into every sc.

8th round: *1sc into each of next 2sc, skip 1, 1sc. *6 times (18st)

9th round: *1sc, skip 1, 1sc. *6 times (12st)

Insert batting.

10th round: *1sc, skip 1. *6 times (6st)

Fasten off.

Ears x2

Start the same way as you did for the head, but with 5sc into the circle.

1st round: 2sc into each of 5sc. (10st)

2nd–4th round: 1sc into every sc.

Fasten off.

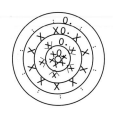

Inside Ears

Use pink fine crochet thread with the 2mm hook.

Start the same way as you did for the head.

1st round: 2sc into each of 6sc. (12st)

2nd round: *1sc, 2sc into next sc. *6 times (18st)

Fasten off.

Body

Start the same way as you did for the head.

1st round: 2sc into each of 6sc. (12st)

2nd round: *1sc, 2sc into next sc. *6 times (18st)

3rd round: *1sc into each of next 2sc, 2sc into next sc. *6 times (24st)

4th–8th round: 1sc into every sc.

9th round: *1sc into each of next 4sc, skip 1, 1sc. *4 times (20st)

10th–13th round: 1sc into every sc.

14th round: *1sc into each of next 8sc, skip 1, 1sc. *Twice (18st)

Insert batting.

15th round: 1sc into every sc.

Fasten off.

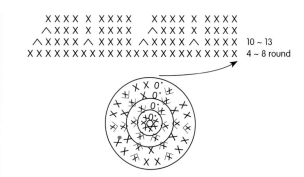

Nose

Start the same way as you did for the head, but with 5sc into the circle.

1st round: 2sc into each of 5sc. (10st)

2nd–3rd round: 1sc into every sc.

4th round: *1sc into each of next 3sc, skip 1, 1sc. *Twice (8st)

5th round: *1sc into every sc.

6th round: 1sc into each of next 2sc, skip 1, 1sc. *Twice (6st)

7th round: 1sc into every sc.

Fasten off.

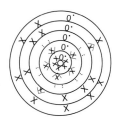

Legs ×2

Start the same way as you did for the head.

1st round: 2sc into each of 6sc. (12st)

2nd round: *1sc, 2sc into next sc. *6 times (18st)

3rd–6th round: 1sc into every sc.

Insert batting.

Fasten off.

Arms ×2

Start the same way as you did for the head.

Keep working with 1sc in round for 4.5cm.

Fasten off.

With 2mm hook and pink crochet thread, pick up 6st.

Fasten off.

Feet ×2

Start the same way as you did for the head, but with 5sc into the circle.

Keep working with 1sc in round for 3cm.

Fasten off.

Toes

With 2mm hook and pink crochet thread, work 4 sl st directly into the tip of the feet.

Tail

Start the same way as you did for the head.

Keep working with 1sc in round for 10cm.

Insert wire with ends curled and fasten off.

Making Up

Sew all parts together as shown in the photograph.

Attach the eyes.

Embroider nose with pink fine crochet thread.

Slow and Steady

Tortoise might be a slow mover, but in a competition for cuteness, he would beat Hare hands down. You can find him crawling around in his favorite spot: among the pebbles in the garden.

Materials

Hook size: 2.5mm

Eyes: 6mm

Moss green yarn (4-ply)

Brown yarn (4-ply)

Dark green yarn

Yellow embroidery thread

Batting

Shell

Section A x7

Start with moss green yarn.

Make a loop with the tail end of the yarn on the right, keeping the ball end on the left.

Pull the ball end through the loop. Make one ch through the loop on the hook you have drawn through to steady the circle. 6sc into the circle and complete with sl st into the first sc.

1st round: Make 1ch to start. 2sc into each of 6sc. Sl st into the first sc to secure. (12st)

2nd round: 1ch, *1sc, 2sc into the next sc. *6 times, then sl st into the first sc to secure. (18st)

3rd round: 1ch, *1sc into each of next 2sc, 2sc into the next sc. *6 times then sl st into the first sc to secure. (24st)

4th round: Change to brown yarn. 1ch, *1sc into each of next 3sc, 2sc into next sc. *6 times (30st)

Fasten off.

Section B x5, triangles

Use moss green yarn.

Make 11 ch.

1ch, 1sc into the second ch from the hook.

1sc into next ch, 1hdc into each of the next 2ch, 1dc, 1 hdc into each of the next 2 ch, 1sc into next ch, finish with 2sc tog.

Fasten off.

Face

Use dark green yarn.

Start the same way as you did for the shell.

1st round: 2sc into each of 6sc. (12st)

2nd round: *1sc, 2sc into next sc. *6 times (18st)

3rd–8th round: 1sc into every sc.

9th round: *1sc, skip 1, 1sc. *6 times (12st)

10th–12th round: 1sc into every sc.

13th round: *1sc into each of next 4sc, skip 1, 1sc. *Twice (10st)

14th–17th round: 1sc into every sc.

Insert batting.

Fasten off.

Legs × 4

Use dark green yarn.

Start the same way as you did for the shell.

1st round: 2sc into each of 6sc. (12st)

Carry on working with sc in round for 4.5cm.

Insert batting.

Fasten off.

Tail

Make 3ch. Keep sc in round for 4 rounds.

*Skip 1, 1sc. *Twice

Fasten off.

Tummy

Use brown yarn.

1st round: 2sc into each of 6sc. (12st)

2nd round: *1sc, 2sc into next sc. *6 times (18st)

3rd round: *1sc into each of next 2sc, 2sc into next sc. *6 times (24st)

4th round: *1sc into each of next 3sc, 2sc into next sc. *6 times (30st)

5th round: *1sc into each of next 4sc, 2sc into next sc. *6 times (36st)

6th round: *1sc into each of next 5sc, 2sc into next sc. *6 times (42st)

7th round: *1sc into each of next 6sc, 2sc into next sc. *6 times (48st)

Insert batting.

8th round: *1sc into each of next 7sc, 2sc into next sc. *6 times (54st)

Fasten off.

Making up

Sew all shell sections together as shown in the photograph.

Sew all parts together as shown in the photograph.

Attach the eyes.

Embroider cute nose and mouth with yellow embroidery thread.

Hamster Heroes

In their hamster cage, these little guys are heroes. They scoot through the tubes and spin their wheels at lightning speed. Use very light pink thread for their tiny paws.

Materials

Hook size: 3mm and 2mm

Eyes: 5mm

Light brown (light gray) yarn

White (cream) yarn

Pink fine crochet thread

Batting

Body

Use light brown (light gray) yarn and the 3mm hook.

Make a loop with the tail end of the yarn on the right, keeping the ball end on the left.

Pull the ball end through the loop. Make one ch through the loop on the hook you have drawn through to steady the circle. 6sc into the circle and complete with sl st into the first sc.

1st round: 2sc into each of 6sc. (12st)

2nd round: *1sc, 2sc into next sc. *6 times (18st)

3rd–6th round: 1sc into every sc.

7th round: *1sc into each of next 8sc, 2sc into next sc. *Twice (20st)

8th–9th round: 1sc into every sc.

After working halfway round, join in white yarn to work tummy section. Cont with white yarn for this section on the following rounds.

10th round: *1sc into each of next 3sc, 2sc into next sc. *5 times (25st)

11th–12th round: 1sc into every sc.

13th round: *1sc into each of next 3sc, skip 1, 1sc. *5 times (20st)

14th round: *1sc into each of next 2sc, skip 1, 1sc. *5 times (15st)

15th round: *1sc, skip 1, 1sc. *5 times (10st)

Insert batting.

16th round: *1sc, skip 1. *5 times (5st)

Fasten off.

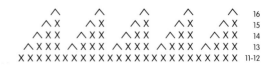

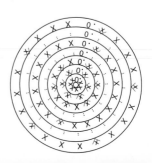

Nose

Use white yarn.

Start the same way as you did for the body.

1st round: 2sc into each of 6sc. (12st)

2nd round: *1sc, 2sc into next sc. *6 times (18st)

3rd–4th round: 1sc into every sc.

Fasten off.

Ears x2

Use light brown (light gray) yarn and the 2mm hook.

Start the same way as you did for the body, but 5sc into the circle.

Join the last sc with the first sc with sl st.

Fasten off.

Arms x2

Use white yarn.

Start the same way as you did for the body, but 4sc into the circle.

Keep working with sc into every sc in round for 1.5cm.

Using a 2mm hook, change to pink fine crochet thread and sc around for 2 rounds.

Fasten off.

Feet x2

Use pink fine crochet thread and the 2mm hook.

Start the same way as you did for the body, but 3sc into the circle.

1st round: 2sc into every sc. (6st)

2nd–4th round: 1sc into every sc.

Making Up

Sew all the parts together as shown in the photograph.

Attach the eyes.

Embroider the nose with pink fine crochet thread.

Horsing Around

This award-winning horse has won lots of show-jumping competitions and has a cabinet full of trophies at home. Although he loves competing, he also enjoys horsing around in the field. Enjoy making lots of rosettes for your prize-winning friend.

Materials

Hook size: 3mm

Eyes: 10mm

White yarn

Brown yarn

Dark brown yarn

Red yarn

Batting

Head

Use white yarn.

Make a loop with the tail end of the yarn on the right, keeping the ball end on the left.

Pull the ball end through the loop. Make one ch through loop on hook you have drawn through to steady the circle. 6sc into the circle and complete with sl st into the first sc.

1st round: 2sc into each of 6sc. (12st)

2nd round: *1sc, 2sc into next sc. *6 times (18st)

3rd round: *1sc into each of next 2sc, 2sc into next sc. *6 times (24st)

4th round: *1sc into each of next 3sc, 2sc into next sc. *6 times (30st)

5th–9th round: 1sc into every sc.

10th round: *1sc into each of next 3sc, skip 1, 1sc. *6 times (24st)

11th–13th round: 1sc into every sc.

14th round: *1sc into each of next 2sc, skip 1, 1sc. *6 times (18st)

15th–16th round: 1sc into every sc.

17th–20th round: Change to brown yarn. 1sc into every sc.

Insert batting.

21st round: *1sc, skip 1, 1sc. *6 times (12st)

22nd round: *1sc, skip 1. *6 times (6st)

Fasten off.

```
      ^       ^       ^       ^       ^       ^    22
    ^ x     ^ x     ^ x     ^ x     ^ x     ^ x    21
  x x x   x x x   x x x   x x x   x x x   x x x    17 ~ 20 (Brown)
  x x x   x x x   x x x   x x x   x x x   x x x    15 ~ 16
 ^ x x  ^ x x  ^ x x  ^ x x  ^ x x  ^ x x          14
 x x x x  x x x x  x x x x  x x x x  x x x x  x x x x  11 ~ 13
^ x x x ^ x x x ^ x x x ^ x x x ^ x x x ^ x x x    10
x x x x x x x x x x x x x x x x x x x x x x x x x x x  6 ~ 9
```

Body

Use white yarn.

Start the same way as for the head.

1st round: 2sc into each of 6sc. (12st)

2nd round: *1sc. 2sc into next sc. *6 times (18st)

3rd round: *1sc into each of next 2sc, 2sc into next sc. *6 times (24st)

4th–16th round: 1sc into every sc.

17th round: *1sc into each of next 2sc, skip 1, 1sc. *6 times (18st)

18th round: *1sc, skip 1, 1sc. *6 times (12st)

Insert batting.

19th round: *1sc, skip 1. *6 times (6st)

Fasten off.

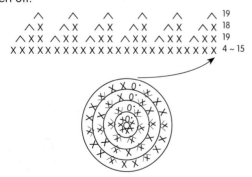

Legs x4

Use white yarn.

Start the same way as you did for the head.

1st round: 2sc into each of 6sc. (12st)

Carry on working sc in round for 7cm.

Change to dark brown yarn and sc for 2 more rounds.

Insert batting.

Then *1sc, skip 1. *6 times (6st).

Fasten off.

Ears x2

Use white yarn.

Start the same way as you did for the head, but with 3sc into the circle.

1st round: 2sc into every sc. (6st)

2nd round: *1sc, 2sc into next sc. *3 times (9st)

3rd round: *1sc into each of next 2sc, 2sc into next sc. *3 times (12st)

4th–5th round: 1sc into every sc.

6th round: *1sc into each of next 2sc, skip 1, 1sc. *3 times. (9st)

7th round: 1sc into every sc.

Fasten off.

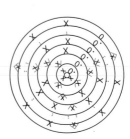

Mane

Use brown yarn.

Make 20 ch. 1 loop st into every ch, and 2 loop st into the last ch.

Work back along other side with 1 loop into every ch.

Fasten off.

```
ᙈᙈᙈᙈᙈᙈᙈᙈᙈᙈᙈᙈᙈᙈᙈᙈᙈᙈᙈᙈ
X X X X X X X X X X X X X X X X X X X X
⊠ X ○○○○○○○○○○○○○○○○○○○○○
X X X X X X X X X X X X X X X X X X X X
ᙡᙡᙡᙡᙡᙡᙡᙡᙡᙡᙡᙡᙡᙡᙡᙡᙡᙡᙡᙡ
```

Neck

Use white yarn.

Make 18ch and join the last ch to the first one with sl st.

Sc in round for 10 rounds.

Fasten off.

Bridle

Use red yarn.

Nose section. Make 15ch and work hdc to end.

Head section. Make 30ch and work hdc to end.

Making Up

Sew all parts together as shown in the photograph, and fasten the bridle to the head.

Make a tassle with brown yarn for the tail and sew it to the body.

Attach the eyes.

Embroider dapple spots with brown yarn.

Peculiar Parrot

This parrot is feeling rather peculiar today. Looking into the mirror, he thinks he's a little off-color. Cheer him up with some brightly colored friends.

Materials

Hook size: 3mm

Eyes: 10mm

Red yarn

White yarn

Blue yarn

Yellow yarn

Black yarn

Batting

Head

Use red yarn.

Make a loop with the tail end of the yarn on the right, keeping the ball end on the left.

Pull the ball end through the loop. Make one ch through the loop on the hook you have drawn through to steady the circle. 6sc into the circle and complete with sl st into the first sc.

1st round: 2sc into each of 6sc. (12st)

2nd round: *1sc, 2sc into next sc. *6 times (18st)

3rd–4th round: 1sc into every sc.

5th round: *1sc into each of next 2sc, 2sc into next sc. *6 times (24st)

6th–8th round: 1sc into every sc.

9th round: 1 ch to start, *insert hook into the first sc and pull out the yarn (enough to make one bubble) 3 times, hook the yarn and pull it all the way through the 3 loops, then hook the yarn and pull it out to secure the bubble.

Insert hook into the 3rd ch and work 1sc into it. Repeat from * for one round.

Insert batting.

Fasten off.

Face

Section A

Use white yarn.

Make 8ch.

1st round: 1ch, 1sc to end. 2sc into the last ch, then work back along the other side to the first ch with sc into each ch.

2nd round: 1ch, 3sc into the first sc. 1sc into each of the next 6sc, 3sc into the next sc, 1sc to return, 3sc into the next sc, 1sc into each of the next 6sc, 3sc into last sc.

Fasten off.

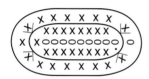

Section B/cheeks x2

Use yellow yarn.

Make a loop and 6sc into the loop.

Fasten off.

Section C/beak rim

Use blue yarn.

Start the same way as you did for the head.

2sc into each of 6sc. (12st)

Fasten off.

Beak

Use black yarn.

Start the same way as you did for the head, but with 4sc into the circle.

2sc into every sc. (8st)

Fasten off.

Body

Use red yarn.

1st round: 2sc into each of 6sc. (12st)

2nd round: *1sc. 2sc into next sc. *6 times (18st)

3rd round: *1sc into each of next 2sc, 2sc into next sc. *6 times (24st)

4th–8th round: 1sc into every sc.

9th round: *1sc into each of next 2sc, skip 1, 1sc. *6 times (18st)

10th–14th round: 1sc into every sc.

Insert batting.

Fasten off.

Wings/tail x3

Use blue yarn.

Start the same way as you did for the head, but with 4sc into the circle.

1st round: 2sc into every sc. (8st)

2nd–3rd round: 1sc into every sc.

4th round: Change to yellow yarn. *1sc, 2sc into next sc. *4 times (12st)

5th–7th round: Change to red yarn. 1sc into every sc.

8th round: *1sc, skip 1, 1sc. *4 times (8st)

Fasten off.

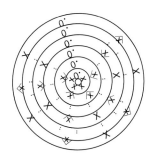

Making Up

Sew all the parts together as shown in the photograph.

Attach the eyes.

Floppy the Fish

Ever feel like you're living in a goldfish bowl? Floppy does. Mostly he's happy to let you watch him swim — he knows how cute he is — but sometimes he gets shy and hides in the leaves and fronds of the aquarium plants.

Materials

Hook size: 3mm

Eyes: 15mm

Red yarn

Orange yarn

White yarn

Black embroidery thread

Batting

Body

Use red yarn.

Make a loop with tail end of yarn on right, keeping ball end on left.

Pull the ball end through loop. Make one ch through the loop on the hook you have drawn through to steady the circle. 6sc into the circle and complete with sl st into the first sc.

1st round: 2sc into each of 6sc. (12st)

2nd round: *1sc, 2sc into next sc. *6 times (18st)

3rd–4th round: 1sc into every sc.

5th round: *1sc into each of next 2sc, 2sc into next sc. *6 times (24st)

6th–11th round: 1sc into every sc.

12th round: *1sc into each of next 2sc, skip 1, 1sc. *6 times (18st)

13th round: *1sc, skip 1, 1sc. *6 times (12st)

Insert batting.

14th round: *1sc, skip 1. *6 times (6st)

Fasten off.

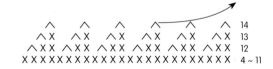

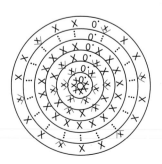

Dorsal Fin

Start the same way as you did for the body.

1st round: 2sc into each of 6sc. (12st)

2nd round: *1sc, 2sc into next sc. *6 times (18st)

Fasten off.

Ventral Fins x2

Start the same way you did for the body.

1st round: 2sc into each of 6sc. (12st)

2nd round: Make 1ch to start. 1sc into the first sc. 2sc into each of next 4sc, 1sc into next sc, join with the first sc with sl st.

Fasten off.

Eyes x2

Start the same way as you did for the body, but with 5sc into the circle.

1st round: 2sc into each of 5sc. (10st)

2nd round: 1sc into every sc.

Fasten off.

Tail

Use white yarn.

Make 25ch.

3ch to start then dc to end and turn.

Keep working on dc to end.

Change to white yarn and 1sc into every st.

Fasten off.

Gather it up along the first row to make the tail shape.

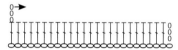

Scales (refer to the diagram)

Use orange yarn.

Make 31ch.

1st row: Make 4 more ch to start. 2dc into the 4th ch from hook.

*Skip next 4ch, 2dc into the next ch, 1ch, 2dc into the same ch you just did dc. Rep from *5 times, then skip next 4ch, 2dc into the next sc, 1ch, 1dc into the same chain you just did dc. Make 3ch for next row.

2nd row: Make 1ch to start. 2dc into the chain in the middle of the shell you made in the first row.* 2dc into the next ch in the middle of the shell, 1ch, 2dc into the same ch you just did dc. Rep from * to end.

Rep those 2 rows again.

Fasten off.

Making Up

Sew all parts together as shown in the photograph.

Attach the eyes.

Embroider the mouth with black embroidery thread.

Slither Snake

Slither Snake is very proud of his purple and yellow stripes, and can often be seen showing them off to the other snakes. Slither likes to wear his red beret slightly to one side. He thinks it makes him look stylish.

Materials

Hook size: 3mm

Eyes: 8mm

Yellow yarn

Purple yarn

Red yarn

Red felt

Wire

Batting

Head

Use purple yarn.

Make a loop with the tail end of the yarn on the right, keeping the ball end on the left.

Pull the ball end through the loop. Make one ch through the loop on the hook you have drawn through to steady the circle. 6sc into the circle and complete with sl st into the first sc.

1st round: 2sc into each of 6sc. (12st)

2nd round: *1sc, 2sc into next sc. *6 times (18st)

3rd round: *1sc into each of next 2sc, 2sc into next sc. *6 times (24st)

4th–5th round: 1sc into every sc.

6th round: *1sc into each of next 2sc, skip 1, 1sc. *6 times (18st)

7th round: *1sc, skip 1, 1sc. *6 times (12st)

Insert batting.

8th round: *1sc, skip 1. *6 times (6st)

Fasten off.

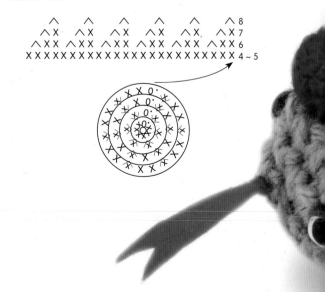

Body

Use yellow yarn.

Make 10ch.

Form a ring joining the last st and the first st with sl st.

1sc into each st. Keep working straight, changing the col for every 2nd round.

Keep working till the stripy tube is long enough to undulate!

Start dec. *1sc into each of next 3sc, skip 1, 1sc. *Twice (8st)

Next round: *1sc into each of next 2sc, skip 1, 1sc. *Twice (6st)

Next round: *1sc, skip 1, 1sc. *Twice (4st)

Insert batting and wire.

Fasten off.

Hat

Use red yarn.

Start with making 6sc into the ring joining the first sc and the last one with sl st.

1st round: 2sc into each of 6sc. (12st)

2nd round: *1sc, 2sc into the next sc. *6 times (18st)

3rd-4th round: 1sc into each sc. (18st)

5th round: *1sc, skip next sc. *6 times (12st)

Insert batting.

Fasten Off.

Making Up

Sew the head to the body as shown in the photograph.

Cut a tongue shape from red felt, and sew it onto the head.

Attach the eyes.

Sew the hat onto the head.

Chapter 2
Into the
Wild

Monkey Mischief

This little monkey likes nothing better than to sit in banana trees and munch away at the tasty fruits until they are all gone. The banana pickers don't like him, but we think he is cuteness itself. Use a long coil for his ears.

Materials

Hook size: 3mm

Eyes: 8mm

Purple yarn

White felt

Black embroidery thread

Batting

Head

Make a loop with the tail end of the yarn on the right, keeping the ball end on the left.

Pull the ball end through the loop. Make one ch through the loop on the hook you have drawn through to steady the circle. 6sc into the circle and complete with sl st into the first sc.

1st round: 2sc into each of 6sc. (12st)

2nd round: *1sc, 2sc into next sc. *6 times (18st)

3rd round: *1sc into each of next 2sc, 2sc into next sc. *6 times (24st)

4th round: *1sc into each of next 3sc, 2sc into next sc. *6 times (30st)

5th round: *1sc into each of next 4sc, 2sc into next sc. *6 times (36st)

6th round: *1sc into each of next 5sc, 2sc into next sc. *6 times (42st)

7th–10th round: 1sc into every sc.

11th round: *1sc into each of next 5sc, skip 1, 1sc. *6 times (36st)

12th round: *1sc into each of next 4sc, skip 1, 1sc. *6 times (30st)

13th round: *1sc into each of next 3sc, skip 1, 1sc. *6 times (24st)

14th round: *1sc into each of next 2sc, skip 1, 1sc. *6 times (18st)

15th round: *1sc, skip 1, 1sc. *6 times (12st)

Insert batting.

16th round: *1sc, skip 1. *6 times (6st)

Fasten off.

```
 ^    ^    ^    ^    ^    ^    ^     16
 ^×   ^×   ^×   ^×   ^×   ^×   ^×    15
 ^×× ^×× ^×× ^×× ^×× ^×× ^××   14
×××× ×××× ×××× ×××× ×××× ××××   13
×××××××××××××××××××××××××××××××   12
×××××××××××××××××××××××××××××××   11
×××××××××××××××××××××××××××××××   7-10
```

Body

Start the same way as you did for the head.

1st round: 2sc into each of 6sc. (12st)

2nd round: *1sc, 2sc into next sc. *6 times (18st)

3rd round: *1sc into each of next 2sc, 2sc into next sc. *6 times (24st)

4th–6th round: 1sc into every sc.

7th round: *1sc into each of next 4sc, skip 1, 1sc. *4 times (20st)

8th–9th round: 1sc into every sc.

Insert batting.

Fasten off.

```
X X X X X  X X X X X  X X X X X  X X X X X   8 ~ 9
∧ X X X X  ∧ X X X X  ∧ X X X X  ∧ X X X X   7
X X X X X X X X X X X X X X X X X X X X X X   4 ~ 6
                                            round
```

Arms x2

Start the same way as you did for the head, but 5sc into the circle.

1st round: 2sc into every sc. (10st)

2nd round: *1sc, 2sc into next sc. *5 times (15st)

3rd–4th round: 1sc into every sc.

5th round: *1sc, skip 1, 1sc. *5 times (10 st)

6th–15th round: 1sc into every sc.

Insert batting.

16th round: *1sc, skip 1. *5 times (5st)

Fasten off.

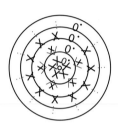

Legs x2

Start the same way as you did for the head, but 5sc into the circle.

1st round: 2sc into every sc. (10st)

2nd–6th round: 1sc into every sc.

Insert batting.

Fasten off.

Ears

Make 50 ch. Sc to end.

Fasten off.

Roll it up and secure the shape with a few stitches.

Making Up

Sew all parts together as shown in the photograph.

Sew white felt patch to the face and embroider the nose with black embroidery thread.

Attach the eyes.

Glum and Glummer

It's a gray day for these little bears. It's raining outside, so they can't go out to play. Nothing but a cuddle, and perhaps a new ribbon, will cheer them up. They're so adorable, and so easy to make, you'll want to create hundreds of them.

Materials

Hook size: 3mm

Eyes: 5mm

Gray yarn

Plastic nose

Ribbon

Black embroidery thread

Batting

Head

Make a loop with the tail end of the yarn on the right, keeping the ball end on left.

Pull the ball end through the loop. Make one ch through the loop on the hook you have drawn through to steady the circle. 6sc into the circle and complete with sl st into the first sc.

1st round: 2sc into each of 6sc. (12st)

2nd round: *1sc, 2sc into next sc. *6 times (18st)

3rd round: *1sc into each of next 2sc, 2sc into next sc. *6 times (24st)

4th round: *1sc into each of next 3sc, 2sc into next sc. *6 times (30st)

5th round: *1sc into each of next 4sc, 2sc into next sc. *6 times (36st)

6th–10th round: 1sc into every sc.

11th round: *1sc into each of next 4sc, skip 1, 1sc. *6 times (30st)

12th round: *1sc into each of next 3sc, skip 1, 1sc. *6 times (24st)

13th round: *1sc into each of next 2sc, skip 1, 1sc. *6 times (18st)

14th round: *1sc, skip 1, 1sc. *6 times (12st)

15th round: *1sc, skip 1. *6 times (6st)

Insert batting.

Fasten off.

```
          ^      ^        ^        ^      ^              15
        ^ x    ^ x      ^ x      ^ x    ^ x      ^ x     14
      ^ x x  ^ x x    ^ x x    ^ x x  ^ x x    ^ x x     13
    ^ x x x ^ x x x ^ x x x ^ x x x ^ x x x ^ x x x      12
  x x x x x x x x x x x x x x x x x x x x x x x x        11
x x x x x x x x x x x x x x x x x x x x x x x x x x x x  6 ~10
```

Ears x2

Start the same way as you did for the head.

1st round: 2sc into each of 6sc. (12st)

2nd–4th round: 1sc into each of 12sc.

Fasten off.   x x x x x x x x x x x x   2 ~ 4

Body

Start the same way as you did for the head.

1st round: 2sc into each of 6sc. (12st)

2nd round: *1sc, 2sc into next sc. *6 times (18st)

3rd round: *1sc into each of next 2sc, 2sc into next sc. *6 times (24st)

4th–11th round: 1sc into every sc.

12th round: *1sc into each of next 2sc, skip 1, 1sc. *6 times (18st)

13th round: *1sc, skip 1, 1sc. *6 times (12st)

Insert batting.

14th round: *1sc, skip 1. *6 times (6st)

Fasten off.

```
        ^        ^        ^        ^        ^        ^        14
      ^ x      ^ x      ^ x      ^ x      ^ x      ^ x        13
    ^ x x    ^ x x    ^ x x    ^ x x    ^ x x    ^ x x        12
  x x x x x x x x x x x x x x x x x x x x x x x x            4 ~ 11
```

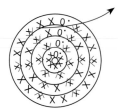

Arms x2

Start the same way as you did for the head.

1st round: 2sc into each of 6sc. (12st)

2nd–6th round: 1sc into every sc. (12st)

7th round: *1sc into next 2sc, skip 1, 1sc. *3 times (9st)

8th–12th round: 1sc into every sc.

13th round: *1sc, skip 1. *3 times (6st)

Insert batting.

Fasten off.

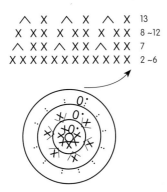

Legs x2

Start the same way as you did for the head.

1st round: 2sc into each of 6sc. (12st)

2nd round: *1sc, 2sc into next sc. *6 times (18st)

3rd–6th round: 1sc into every sc.

7th round: *1sc, skip 1, 1sc. *6 times (12st)

8th–10th round: 1sc into every sc.

11th round: *1sc into next 2sc, skip 1, 1sc. *3 times (9st)

12th round: *1sc, skip 1. *3 times (6st)

Insert batting.

Fasten off.

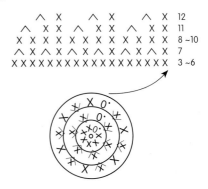

Making Up

Sew all parts together as shown in the photograph.

Attach the eyes and nose.

Embroider the mouth and eyebrows with black embroidery thread.

Tie the ribbon around the bear's neck.

Trunks and Tusks

If you let him, this circus elephant will show you all his tricks. He can stand on one leg, jump through hoops, and balance balls on the end of his trunk. Yet he is so cute, he doesn't need tricks to impress! Make his ears extra floppy for maximum cuteness.

Materials

Hook size: 3mm

Eyes: 10mm

Heather gray yarn

White felt

Batting

Head

Make a loop with the tail end of the yarn on the right, keeping the ball end on the left.

Pull the ball end through the loop. Make one ch through the loop on the hook you have drawn through to steady the circle. 6sc into the circle and complete with sl st into the first sc.

1st round: 2sc into each of 6sc. (12st)

2nd round: *1sc, 2sc into next sc. *6 times (18st)

3rd round: *1sc into each of next 2sc, 2sc into next sc. *6 times (24st)

4th round: *1sc into each of next 3sc, 2sc into next sc. *6 times (30st)

5th–8th round: 1sc into every sc.

9th round: *1sc into each of next 3sc, skip 1, 1sc. *6 times (24st)

10th round: *1sc into each of next 2sc, skip 1, 1sc. *6 times (18st)

11th round: *1sc, skip 1, 1sc. *6 times (12st)

Insert batting.

12th round: *1sc, skip 1. *6 times (6st)

Fasten off.

Body

Start the same way as you did for the head.

1st round: 2sc into each of 6sc. (12st)

2nd round: *1sc, 2sc into next sc. *6 times (18st)

3rd round: *1sc into each of next 2sc, 2sc into next sc. *6 times (24st)

4th round: *1sc into each of next 3sc, 2sc into next sc. *6 times (30st)

5th–8th round: 1sc into every sc.

9th round: *1sc into each of next 3sc, skip 1, 1sc. *6 times (24st)

10th–13th round: 1sc into every sc.

14th round: *1sc into each of next 2sc, skip 1, 1sc. *6 times (18st)

15th–16th round: 1sc into every sc.

Insert batting.

Fasten off.

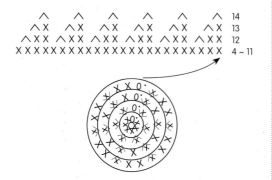

Ears x2

Start the same way as you did for the head.

1st round: 2sc into each of 6sc. (12st)

2nd round: *1sc, 2sc into next sc. *6 times (18st)

3rd round: *1sc into each of next 2sc, 2sc into next sc. *6 times (24st)

4th–8th round: 1sc into every sc.

Fasten off.

Gather it up to make an ear shape.

Arms x2

Start the same way as the head.

1st round: 2sc into each of 6sc. (12st)

Keep working sc in round for 4.5cm.

Insert batting.

Fasten off.

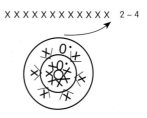

Legs x2

Start the same way as you did for the head.

1st round: 2sc into each of 6sc. (12st)

Keep working sc in round for 5.5cm.

Insert batting.

Fasten off.

Trunk

Make 6ch.

1sc into each ch.

Keep working in round for 6cm.

Fasten off.

Making Up

Sew all the parts together as shown in the photograph.

Cut white felt for tummy, legs, and arms and stitch it onto the body.

Attach the eyes.

Baby Panda

Cute little Panda loves bamboo. Deep in the misty forests of China, Panda will sit and munch on his favorite plant all day long. Panda is kind of shy, but give him some bamboo and he will be your friend for life.

Materials

Hook size: 3mm

Eyes: 8mm

Black yarn

White yarn

Plastic nose

Black embroidery thread

Batting

Head

Use white yarn.

Make a loop with the tail end of the yarn on the right, keeping the ball end on the left.

Pull the ball end through the loop. Make one ch through the loop on the hook you have drawn through to steady the circle. 6sc into the circle and complete with sl st into the first sc.

1st round: 2sc into each of 6sc. (12st)

2nd round: *1sc, 2sc into next sc. *6 times (18st)

3rd round: *1sc into each of next 2sc, 2sc into next sc. *6 times (24st)

4th round: *1sc into each of next 3sc, 2sc into next sc. *6 times (30st)

5th–7th round: 1sc into every sc.

8th round: *1sc into each of next 3sc, skip 1, 1sc. *6 times (24st)

9th round: *1sc into each of next 2sc, skip 1, 1sc. *6 times (18st)

10th round: *1sc, skip 1, 1sc. *6 times (12st)

Insert batting.

11th round: *1sc, skip 1. *6 times (6st)

Fasten off.

Body

Use white yarn.

Start the same way as you did for the head.

1st round: 2sc into each of 6sc. (12st)

2nd round: *1sc, 2sc into next sc. *6 times (18st)

3rd round: *1sc into each of next 2sc, 2sc into next sc. *6 times (24st)

4th–5th round: 1sc into every sc.

6th round: *1sc into each of next 3sc, 2sc into next sc. *6 times (30st)

7th–10th round: 1sc into every sc.

11th round: *1sc into each of next 3sc, skip 1, 1sc. *6 times (24st)

12th–13th round: 1sc into every sc.

14th–15th round: Change to black yarn. 1sc into every sc.

Insert batting.

16th round: *1sc into each of next 2sc, skip 1, 1sc. *6 times (18st)

Fasten off.

Nose

Use white yarn.

Start the same way as you did for the head.

1st round: 2sc into each of 6sc. (12st)

2nd round: *1sc, 2sc into next sc. *6 times (18st)

3rd–5th round: 1sc into every sc.

Fasten off.

Ears x2

Use black yarn.

Start the same way as you did for the head.

1st round: 2sc into each of 6sc. (12st)

2nd–4th round: 1sc into every sc.

Fasten off.

Arms x2

Use black yarn.

Start the same way as you did for the head.

1st round: 2sc into each of 6sc. (12st)

2nd–5th round: 1sc into every sc.

6th round: *1sc into each of next 2sc, skip 1, 1sc. *3 times (9st)

7th–10th round: 1sc into every sc.

Insert batting.

Fasten off.

Legs x2

Use black yarn.

Start the same way as you did for the head.

1st round: 2sc into each of 6sc. (12st)

Keep working in sc for 5.5cm.

*1sc, skip 1. *6 times

Insert batting.

Fasten off.

Tail

Use black yarn.

Start the same way as you did for the head.

1st round: 2sc into each of 6sc. (12st)

2nd–3rd round: 1sc into every sc.

Fasten off.

Making Up

Sew all parts together as shown in the photograph.

Attach the eyes and nose.

Embroider mouth with black embroidery thread.

Chapter 3
In the Ocean

Mr. Octopus

Mr. Octopus can often be seen gliding along the coral reef admiring the fishes and the pretty shells. Mr. Octopus, with his eight legs, takes a while to make, but it's worth it when you see him smiling back at you!

Materials

Hook size: 3mm

Eyes: 10mm

Dark blue yarn

Jewelry wire

Red embroidery thread

Batting

Head

Make a loop with the tail end of the yarn on the right, keeping the ball end on the left.

Pull the ball end through loop. Make one ch through loop on hook you have drawn through to steady the circle. 6sc into the circle and complete with sl st into the first sc.

1st round: 2sc into each of 6sc. (12st)

2nd round: *1sc, 2sc into next sc. *6 times (18st)

3rd round: *1sc into each of next 2sc, 2sc into next sc. *6 times (24st)

4th round: *1sc into each of next 3sc, 2sc into next sc. *6 times (30st)

5th round: *1sc into each of next 4sc, 2sc into next sc. *6 times (36st)

6th–11th round: 1sc into every sc.

12th round: *1sc into each of next 4sc, skip 1, 1sc. *6 times (30st)

13th–17th round: 1sc into every sc.

18th round: *1sc into each of next 3sc, skip 1, 1sc. *6 times (24st)

19th–20th round: 1sc into every sc.

21st round: *1sc into each of next 2sc, skip 1, 1sc. *6 times (18st)

15th round: *1sc, skip 1, 1sc. *6 times (12st)

Insert batting.

16th round: *1sc, skip 1. *6 times (6st)

Fasten off.

Legs x8

Start the same way as you did for the head, but with 4sc into a circle.

1st round: 2sc into each of 4sc. (8st)

Keep working 1sc into every sc until it gets long enough for the octopus (10cm for this sample).

Fasten off.

Insert wire and batting into each leg (see illustrations.)

Making Up

Sew all parts together as shown in the photograph.

And don't forget to attach his eyes and embroider his smile with red embroidery thread.

Dolphin Days

This clever dolphin spends his days in shallow tropical seas, playing games with his ball and swimming with his fellow dolphins. Once you have mastered the art of dolphin-making, you'll want to make whole schools of them.

Materials

Hook size: 3mm

Eyes: 10mm

Light gray yarn

Batting

Body

Make a loop with the tail end of the yarn on the right, keeping the ball end on the left.

Pull the ball end through the loop. Make one ch through the loop on the hook you have drawn through to steady the circle. 6sc into the circle and complete with sl st into the first sc.

1st round: 2sc into each of 6sc. (12st)

2nd–4th round: 1sc into every sc.

5th round: *1sc into each of next 2sc, 2sc into next sc. *4 times (16st)

6th–9th round: 1sc into every sc.

10th round: *1sc into each of next 3sc, 2sc into next sc. *4 times (20st)

11th–12th round: 1sc into every sc.

13th round: *1sc into each of next 4sc, 2sc into next sc. *4 times (24st)

14th round: *1sc into each of next 5sc, 2sc into next sc. *4 times (28st)

15th round: *1sc into each of next 6sc, 2sc into next sc. *4 times (32st)

16th–17th round: 1sc into every sc.

18th round: *1sc into each of next 6sc, skip 1, 1sc. *4 times (28st)

19th round: *1sc into each of next 5sc, skip 1, 1sc. *4 times (24st)

20th round: *1sc into each of next 4sc, skip 1, 1sc. *4 times (20st)

21st round: *1sc into each of next 3sc, skip 1, 1sc. *4 times (16st)

22nd round: *1sc into each of next 2sc, skip 1, 1sc. *4 times (12st)

Insert batting.

23rd round: *1sc, skip 1. *6 times (6st)

Fasten off.

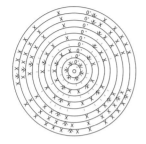

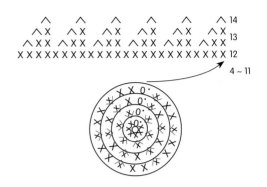

Fold in half and sew around the edge.

Nose

Start the same way as you did for the head.

1st round: 2sc into each of 6sc. (12st)

2nd round: *1sc, 2sc into next sc. *6 times (18st)

3rd–5th round: 1sc into every sc.

Fasten off.

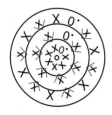

Ventral fins x2

Start the same way as you did for the head.

1st round: 2sc into each of 6sc. (12st)

2nd round: *1sc, 2sc into next sc. *6 times (18st)

3rd round: *1sc into each of next 2sc, 2sc into next sc. *6 times (24st)

Fasten off.

Tail x2

Start the same way as you did for the head, but with 4sc in a circle.

1st round: 2sc into each of 4sc. (8st)

2nd round: *1sc, 2sc into next sc. *4 times (12st)

3rd round: *1sc into each of next 2sc, 2sc into next sc. *4 times (16st)

4th round: *1sc into each of next 3sc, 2sc into next sc. *4 times (20st)

5th round: *1sc into each of next 4sc, 2sc into next sc. *4 times (24st)

Fasten off.

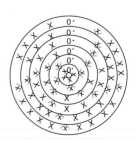

Fold in half and sew around the edge.

Making Up

Sew ventral fins, tail, and nose to the body.

Attach the eyes.

Chapter 4
Flippers
and Wings

Little Blue

Little Blue is the smallest member of the penguin family, and a delightful addition to your amigurumi world. By day he runs down to the sea to catch fish; by night he settles into his cozy burrow with his penguin friends. Use mohair fur to make him extra fluffy.

Materials

Hook size: 2.3mm

Eyes: 10mm

Light blue mohair

White mohair

Yellow fine crochet thread

Black yarn

Batting

Head

Use blue mohair.

Make a loop with the tail end of the yarn on the right, keeping the ball end on the left.

Pull the ball end through the loop. Make one ch through loop on the hook you have drawn through to steady the circle. 6sc into the circle and complete with sl st into the first sc.

1st round: 2sc into each of 6sc. (12st)

2nd round: *1sc, 2sc into next sc. *6 times (18st)

3rd round: *1sc into each of next 2sc, 2sc into next sc. *6 times (24st)

4th round: *1sc into each of next 3sc, 2sc into next sc. *6 times (30st)

5th–11th round: 1sc into every sc.

Insert batting.

Fasten off.

Face

Use white mohair.

Start the same way as you did for the head.

1st round: 2sc into each of 6sc. (12st)

2nd round: *1sc, 2sc into next sc. *6 times (18st)

3rd round: *1sc into each of next 2sc, 2sc into next sc. *6 times (24st)

Fasten off.

Body

Use blue mohair.

Start the same way as you did for the head.

1st round: 2sc into each of 6sc. (12st)

2nd round: *1sc, 2sc into next sc. *6 times (18st)

3rd round: *1sc into each of next 2sc, 2sc into next sc. *6 times (24st)

4th round: *1sc into each of next 3sc, 2sc into next sc. *6 times (30st)

5th round: *1sc into each of next 4sc, 2sc into next sc. *6 times (36st)

6th round: *1sc into each of next 5sc, 2sc into next sc. *6 times (42st)

7th–13th round: 1sc into every sc.

14th round: *1sc into each of next 5sc, skip 1, 1sc. *6 times (36st)

15th round: *1sc into each of next 4sc, skip 1, 1sc. *6 times (30st)

Insert batting.

16th round: 1sc into every sc.

Fasten off.

Arms x2

Use blue mohair.

Start the same way as you did for the head, but with 3sc in a circle.

1st round: 2sc into each of 3sc. (6st)

2nd round: *1sc, 2sc into next sc. *3 times (9st)

3rd round: *1sc into each of next 2sc, 2sc into next sc. *3 times (12st)

4th–7th round: 1sc into every sc.

Fasten off.

Feet x2

Use black yarn.

Start the same way as you did for the head.

1st round: 2sc into each of 6sc. (12st)

2nd–3rd round: 1sc into every sc.

Fasten off.

Beak

Use yellow crochet thread.

Start the same way as you did for the head.

1st round: 2sc into each of 6sc. (12st)

2nd–4th round: 1sc into every sc.

Fasten off.

Tummy

Use white mohair.

Start the same way as you did for the head.

1st round: 2sc into each of 6sc. (12st)

2nd round: *1sc, 2sc into next sc. *6 times (18st)

3rd round: *1sc into each of next 2sc, 2sc into next sc. *6 times (24st)

4th round: *1sc into each of next 3sc, 2sc into next sc. *6 times (30st)

5th round: *1sc into each of next 4sc, 2sc into next sc. *6 times (36st)

Fasten off.

Making Up

Sew all parts together as shown in the photograph.

Attach the eyes.

Embroider the face with light blue mohair.

Blind as a Barn Bat

Barn Bat sleeps all day in the barn, folded up snugly in her wings. She likes to hide in the shadows when the sun is out, but loves to fly around the neighborhood at night. Use pink felt for her ears and wing tips.

Materials

Hook size: 2.3mm

Eyes: 6mm

Brown yarn (4-ply)

Light brown felt

Light pink felt

Pink embroidery thread

Batting

Head

Make a loop with the tail end of the yarn on the right, keeping the ball end on the left.

Pull the ball end through the loop. Make one ch through the loop on the hook you have drawn through to steady the circle. 6sc into the circle and complete with sl st into the first sc.

1st round : 2sc into each of 6sc. (12st)

2nd round: *1sc, 2sc into next sc. *6 times (18st)

3rd round: *1sc into each of next 2sc, 2sc into next sc. *6 times (24st)

4th round: *1sc into each of next 3sc, 2sc into next sc. *6 times (30st)

5th round: *1sc into each of next 4sc, 2sc into next sc. *6 times (36st)

6th round: *1sc into each of next 5sc, 2sc into next sc. *6 times (42st)

7th–10th round: 1sc into every sc.

11th round: *1sc into each of next 5sc, skip 1, 1sc. *6 times (36st)

12th round: *1sc into each of next 4sc, skip 1, 1sc. *6 times (30st)

13th round: *1sc into each of next 3sc, skip 1, 1sc. *6 times (24st)

14th round: *1sc into each of next 2sc, skip 1, 1sc. *6 times (18st)

15th round: *1sc, skip 1, 1sc. *6 times (12st)

Insert batting.

16th round: *1sc, skip 1. *6 times (6st)

Fasten off.

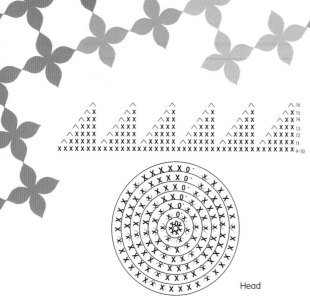

Body

Start the same way as you did for the head.

1st round: 2sc into each of 6sc. (12st)

2nd round: *1sc, 2sc into next sc. *6 times (18st)

3rd round: *1sc into each of next 2sc, 2sc into next sc. *6 times (24st)

4th round: *1sc into each of next 3sc, 2sc into next sc. *6 times (30st)

5th–8th round: 1sc into every sc.

9th round: *1sc into each of next 3sc, skip 1, 1sc. *6 times (24st)

10th round: *1sc into each of next 2sc, skip 1, 1sc. *6 times (18st)

11th round: *1sc, skip 1, 1sc. *6 times (12st)

Insert batting.

12th round: *1sc, skip 1. *6 times (6st)

Fasten off.

Making Up

Sew the head and body together as shown in the photograph.

Cut out the wings from the brown felt.

Cut out the ears, nose, and hands from the light pink felt.

Attach all the felt features as shown in the photograph.

Don't forget to attach the eyes and embroider his mouth with pink embroidery thread.

Chapter 5

In the
Garden

Slippy and Slimy

Slippy and Slimy are the very best of friends. They can often be found gossiping about the other snails in the mushroom patch at the bottom of the garden. Add extra stuffing to their shells to make them harder to the touch, and don't forget their feelers!

Materials

Hook size: 3mm

Eyes: 6mm

Cream (or blue) yarn

Brown (or green) yarn

Red embroidery thread

Batting

Body

Use cream (or blue) yarn.

Make a loop with the tail end of the yarn on the right, keeping the ball end on the left.

Pull the ball end through the loop. Make one ch through the loop on the hook you have drawn through to steady the circle. 6sc into the circle and complete with sl st into the first sc.

1st round: 2sc into each of 6sc. (12st)

2nd round: *1sc, 2sc into next sc. *6 times (18st)

3rd–10th round: 1sc into every sc.

11th round: *1sc into each of next 7sc, skip 1, 1sc. *Twice (16st)

12th–17th round: 1sc into every sc.

18th round: *1sc into each of next 6sc, skip 1, 1sc. *Twice (14st)

19th–22nd round: 1sc into every sc.

23rd round: *1sc into each of next 5sc, skip 1, 1sc. *Twice (12st)

24th round: *1sc into each of next 2sc, skip 1, 1sc. *3 times (9st)

Insert batting.

25th round: *1sc, skip 1, 1sc. *3 times (6st)

Fasten off.

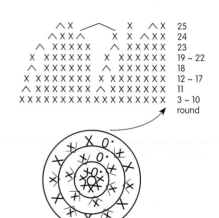

Shell

Use brown (or green) yarn.

Make 40ch. Keep working in sc for 3 rows.

Fasten off.

Roll it up and secure the shell shape with stitches.

Making Up

When you stuff the body, make sure that there is less stuffing toward the tail section, as the tail needs to be floppy to make it easy to shape.

Sew the shell to the body as shown in the photograph.

Attach the eyes.

Also, don't forget to give your snails feelers using a scrap of yarn!

Pond Frog

Life is sweet for Pond Frog. He can leap 100 feet if he wants to, so he finds it easy to get around. Mostly, though, he likes to sit on the lily pad, frightening away the other pond life. We think he is too cute to be scary!

Materials

Hook size: 3mm

Eyes: 15mm

Dark green yarn

Yellow embroidery thread

Batting

Head

Make a loop with the tail end of the yarn on the right, keeping the ball end on the left.

Pull the ball end through the loop. Make one ch through the loop on the hook you have drawn through to steady the circle. 6sc into the circle and complete with sl st into the first sc.

1st round: 2sc into each of 6sc. (12st)

2nd round: *1sc, 2sc into next sc. *6 times (18st)

3rd round: *1sc into each of next 2sc, 2sc into next sc. *6 times (24st)

4th round: *1sc into each of next 3sc, 2sc into next sc. *6 times (30st)

5th–6th round: 1sc into every sc.

7th round: *1sc into each of next 3sc, skip 1, 1sc. *6 times (24st)

8th round: *1sc into each of next 2sc, skip 1, 1sc. *6 times (18st)

9th round: *1sc, skip 1, 1sc. *6 times (12st)

Insert batting.

10th round: *1sc, skip 1. *6 times (6st)

Fasten off.

Body

Start the same way as you did for the head.

1st round: 2sc into each of 6sc. (12st)

2nd round: *1sc, 2sc into next sc. *6 times (18st)

3rd round: *1sc into each of next 2sc, 2sc into next sc. *6 times (24st)

4th round: *1sc into each of next 3sc, 2sc into next sc. *6 times (30st)

5th–9th round: 1sc into every sc.

10th round: *1sc into each of next 4sc, skip 1, 1sc. *5 times (25st)

11th–12th round: 1sc into every sc.

13th round: *1sc into each of next 3sc, skip 1, 1sc. *5 times (20st)

14th–15th round: 1sc into every sc.

Insert batting.

16th round: *1sc into each of next 2sc, skip 1, 1sc. *5 times (15st)

Fasten off.

Eyes x2

Start the same way as you did for the head.

1st round: 2sc into each of 6sc. (12st)

2nd–6th round: 1sc into every sc.

Fasten off.

Legs x2

Start the same way as you did for the head.

1st round: 2sc into each of 6sc. (12st)

2nd round: *1sc, 2sc into next sc. *6 times (18st)

3rd–5th round: 1sc into every sc.

Insert batting.

Fasten off.

Feet x2

Start the same way as you did for the head.

1st round: 2sc into each of 6sc. (12st)

2nd round: Make 3ch, 1sc into the next sc, then make 3ch again.

Repeat this to make 3 loops.

Hands x2

Start the same way as you did for the head.

Make 3ch, 1sc into the next sc, then make 3ch again.

Repeat this to make 3 loops.

Making Up

Sew all parts together as shown in the photograph.

Attach the eyes.

Embroider nose and mouth with yellow embroidery thread.

Lazy Ladybugs

During the long, hot summer, these ladybugs get too lazy to fly and like to find nice soft leaves to doze away on. Use bright red wool for their backs so that they are visible against the dark green leaves.

Materials

Hook size: 3mm

Eyes: 7mm

Red yarn

Black yarn

Batting

Body

Use red yarn.

Make a loop with the tail end of the yarn on the right, keeping the ball end on the left.

Pull the ball end through the loop. Make one ch through the loop on the hook you have drawn through to steady the circle. 6sc into the circle and complete with sl st into the first sc.

1st round: 2sc into each of 6sc. (12st)

2nd round: *1sc, 2sc into next sc. *6 times (18st)

3rd round: *1sc into each of next 2sc, 2sc into next sc. *6 times (24st)

4th round: *1sc into each of next 3sc, 2sc into next sc. *6 times (30st)

5th–6th round: 1sc into every sc.

7th round: Change to black yarn. *1sc into each of next 3sc, skip 1, 1sc. *6 times (24st)

8th round: *1sc into each of next 2sc, skip 1, 1sc. *6 times (18st)

9th round: *1sc, skip 1, 1sc. *6 times (12st)

Insert batting.

10th round: *1sc, skip 1. *6 times (6st)

Fasten off.

Face

Use black yarn.

Start the same way as you did for the body.

1st round: 2sc into each of 6sc. (12st)

2nd round: *1sc, 2sc into next sc. *6 times (18st)

3rd round: 1sc into every sc.

4th round: *1sc, skip 1, 1sc. *6 times (12st)

5th round: *1sc, skip 1. *6 times (6st)

Fasten off.

Dots x4

Use black yarn.

Start the same way as you did for the body.

Fasten off.

Making Up

Sew the face onto the body as shown in the photograph.

Attach dots to the body, eyes to the head, and embroider a line down the middle with black yarn.

Little Ladies

If you don't have time to make a full-size ladybug, these mini versions are ideal. Pick up some clips from the sewing store, attach them to the little ladies, and make yourself some lovely brooches!

Body

Use red yarn.

6sc into the loop to start, 2sc into each st. (12st)

1sc into every st for 2 rounds, then change color to black and 1sc into every st for another round.

Start dec. 1sc and skip next sc to end. (6st)

Insert batting and embroider the details!

If you attach a pin to the back, you can wear it as a brooch!

Resources

Enter the super cute world of amigurumi. The following is a list of tried and tested retailers and suppliers that can help you on your mission to fill your life with cuteness.

Yarns

Blue Sky Alpacas, Inc.

P.O. Box 88

Cedar, MN 55011

Brown Sheep Yarn Company

10062 County Road

Mitchell, NE 69357

Knitting Fever, Inc.

www.knittingfever.com

Knitty City

208 W. 79th St.

New York, NY 10024

www.knittycity.com

Lion Brand Yarns

135 Kero Road

Carlstadt, NJ 07072

www.lionbrand.com

Misti Alpaca

P.O.Box 2532

Glen Ellyn, Illinois

60138

www.mistalpaca.com

Patons

320 Livingstone Avenue South

Listowel, ON

N4W 3H3

Hooks

Clover

www.clover-usa.com

Herrshners

www.herrschners.com

Useful Information

If you are stuck for an idea or missing tools and materials, there is a serious online community support network of crochet and amigurumi enthusiasts. Check out *The Crochet Guild of America* (*www.crochet.org*) for crochet news, links to resources, and tips and advice. Try *Etsy* (*www.etsy.com*) for patterns, accessories, books, and all your other amigurumi needs.

Index

A
abbreviations 11
Amigurumi 6–7
Anime 7
assembling the animals 18

B
Baby Panda 98–101
Bad Budgies 44–47
bat 118–121
beaks 8, 47, 72
birds 44–47
Bad Budgies 44–47
    Little Blue 114–117
    Peculiar Parrot 70–73
Blind as a Barn Bat 118–121
Bouncing Bunnies 48–53
brooches 138–139
budgie 44–47
buttons 36

C
chains
    counting 13
    making 12
    ring 15
color 20
Crazy Kitten 40–43
crochet hooks 8
    holding 12
    sizes 11
Cute Kitten 36–39

D
designing animals 20
discs, flat 18
doll festivals 6
Dolphin Days 108–111

E
ears, felt 118–121
egg shapes 19, 20
elephant 94–97
embroidery 47, 57
eyes 19

F
faces and facial expressions 19
fastening off 18
feelers 126–127
fine crochet cotton lace thread 8
fish 74–77
Floppy Ears 24–27
Floppy the Fish 74–77
Fluffy Fur 28–31
frog 128–131

G
Glum and Glummer 88–93
goldfish 74–77

H
half spheres 19, 20
half-treble 16
Hamster Heroes 62–65

head to body size ratio 19
Hina Matsuri 6
Horsing Around 66–69

I
in the round, working 13–15
increasing 14

J
Japanese craft tradition 6
joining parts 18

K
Kawaii culture 7
kittens
    Crazy Kitten 40–43
    Cute Kitten 36–39

L
ladybugs 132–139
Lazy Ladybugs 132–137
limbs
    attaching 18
    wired 104–107
Little Blue 114–117
Little Ladies 138–139

M
manes 69
Manga 7
mohair 28–31, 50, 114–117
Monkey Mischief 84–87
mood, conveying 19
mouths 19

Mr. Octopus 104–107
mushroom 124–127

N
needles 8
noses 19
    button 36
    embroidered 57
    plastic 24

O
octopus 104–107
Odairi-sami/Ohina-sama dolls 6

P
parrot 70–73
Peculiar Parrot 70–73
penguin 114–117
pins 8
Pond Frog 128–131
posture 20
puppies
    Floppy Ears 24–27
    Fluffy Fur 28–31
    Wagging Tails 32–35

R
rabbit 48–53
Rat Attack 54–57
reading crochet patterns 11

S
sausage shapes 19, 20
single crochet 14, 16

size 20

sketching 20

slip stitch 13, 14

slipknot 12

Slippy and Slimy 24–27

Slither Snake 78–81

Slow and Steady 58–60

snail 24–27

snake 78–81

spheres 18, 20

split stitch markers 8

stitches 12–17

T

techniques 12–17

texture 19, 20

tongue 78

tools and equipment 8

tortoise 58–60

treble crochet 16

Trunks and Tusks 94–97

tweezers 8

U

US and UK crochet terms 11

W

Wagging Tails 32–35

wings 46–47, 73

felt 118–121

wire, craft 8, 78–81, 104

Y

yarn over hook 14

yarns 8

choosing 19

holding 12

mohair 28–31, 50, 114–117